ON JOYCE

NCQ TITLES

Legal Fictions
Politics & Letters
On Yeats: Upon a House
Drama & Democracy
Locating Theology
Time Pieces
Critical Paranoia
On Joyce: 3 easy essays
On Eliot
Literary Conversions

Film texts

A Trip to Rome
A Short Break in Budapest
Magic in Prague
A Week in Venice
Four Days in Athens
The Last Priest of Horus
WWW: the weekend that warped the world

Play texts

Darwin: an evolutionary entertainment
Strange Meetings & Shorts

Eliotics

Forthcoming

Rubbishing Hockney & other reviews
On Collecting Walter Benjamin
Autobiography & Class Consciousness
Considering Canterbury Cathedral

Though each can be read independently, these NCQ publications, taken together, comprise a single hyper-text collection.

ON JOYCE

THREE EASY ESSAYS

Bernard Sharratt

New Crisis Quarterly
2015

NEW CRISIS QUARTERLY

ncq@newcrisisquarterly.myzen.co.uk

First published 2015

ISBN : 978-1-910956-01-4

For
all the
O'Connors
who left

CONTENTS

FOREWORD

This small book brings together three deliberately short and introductory essays which offer complementary perspectives upon the work of James Joyce. They derive from university courses I taught intermittently on Joyce and Yeats (and other Irish writers) in several different contexts, over many years, and the enjoyment was always that of introducing readers to the sheer fun and exhilaration of Joyce's writing. Many students, however, ranging from those in WEA classes to postgraduates, tended to be alarmed or even put off by what seemed to be (and is) a formidable body of Joyce scholarship which they felt they had somehow to tackle first.

I recognise there was a definite relation between the enormous growth of scholarly apparatus and commentary and some facets of Joyce's own work, which I partly explore in relation to *Portrait*, but it was perhaps made worse by the fierce copyright grip long exercised by the Joyce Estate. If you had to pay considerable fees just to quote Joyce, and to make sure you were quoting the 'correct' text, then only dedicated scholars, making a career out of Joyce, were likely to pay those fees, either relying upon an academic publisher's advance payment or hoping for a spin-off in terms of enhanced promotions and pay. So there have been acres of scholarly output from professional Joyceans, but relatively little in the way of accessible literary criticism, as distinct from conscientious annotation or introductory guides, since such low-level pedagogic offerings were not very prestigious in the highly professionalised and competitive world of the Joyce industry.

I recall that when I was an undergraduate, over fifty years ago, I happened to run into a Truly Awesome & Eminent Joyce Scholar, outside the Martello Tower in Dún Laoghaire, which had just then been turned into a Joyce Museum. He asked if I too was a visiting Joyce scholar. "No," I replied, "just an undergraduate. I'm currently scaling the North Face of *Finnegans Wake*." He didn't ask if I was enjoying it, still less eagerly offer to discuss what I was making of it. Instead: "Oh. Which edition?" "Er, a Random House paperback." "Huh," he snorted, "that's got hundreds of misprints." And that was the end of the exchange.

Now that Joyce is at last out of copyright (but see the cautionary note below) and I'm happily retired and don't care (I never did) about scholarly reputation or career, and since print-on-demand opportunities mean that nobody is necessarily dependent upon a publisher's advance or on royalties, I finally reckoned it would be relatively harmless and perhaps even still useful to publish these three easy essays.

The first dates from a moment teaching in Barbados in the mid-1970s when students were partly intrigued by the overlay between the situation in Ireland and the West Indies' own fairly recent struggle for independence, but rather sceptical about the value of studying Irish literature in that context. I wanted to make a case which Joyce himself had suggested: that developing an adequate language for one-self was a crucial step in one's cultural emancipation and therefore a contribution to a larger political liberation. Not that my lecture on *Dubliners* was that crudely, and perhaps tactlessly, explicit, but the case is there. Several years later Hugh Kenner took a similar line about how Joyce constructs his 'voices' in *Dubliners* and memorably coined the phrase 'the Uncle Charles Principle', but Kenner's critical case went in a rather different and somewhat a-political direction. Since Kenner's work has been an exceptional example of deep scholarship combined with infectiously enthusiastic critical response, I have gratefully now added a reference to Kenner's phrase which I and my students would indeed have found helpful at the time.

The second essay, on *Portrait*, stems from the mid-1980s when I was teaching a long-running course on Yeats and Joyce at the University of Kent in England together with, at various times, John Kelly and Declan Kiberd, both admirable scholars who taught me much. This essay derives from a lecture I used to give on why Joyce's work had become so acceptable a focus for precisely such university courses, with some attempt to draw out connections between my students' own more general cultural situation and that of Stephen Dedalus, with an eye particularly on their relation to the broadcast media which had to some extent displaced 'literature' and even threatened its cultural importance.

The third essay is a variant on, or application of, the suggestion in the *Portrait* essay concerning two ways of reading Joyce. It was originally improvised for a literary group in Krakow in the early 1980s (an interesting time to be in Poland), who had asked for an accessible talk on *Ulysses*. I therefore offered a kind of reading (as in 'poetry reading') of some sections of *Ulysses* compressed into a paraphrastic commentary, together with a brief overview of one basic structural principle of the novel, with an eye on the fact that most of my Polish audience were deeply familiar, as Joyce was, with problems in Catholic theological doctrine, an aspect of his work somewhat less familiar to my English students.

I have not attempted an introductory essay on *Finnegans Wake*, but I remember with delight a quite brilliant and marvellously accessible lecture on *FW* at Barbados by the Guyanese poet Mark McWatt, so such an introduction is indeed possible. I would only suggest that anyone fresh to the *Wake* might initially ignore the ever more formidable labyrinth of Joycean scholarship on that extraordinary text, and simply *listen* to it in the magnificent reading by Patrick Healy available on *www.ubu.com* — it's a genuine joy!

Allow me a note on the imprint under which this book is published: *New Crisis Quarterly* (*NCQ*) was an extremely short-lived periodical, its first, only, and farewell issue appearing in 1984, under the guise of *The Literary Labyrinth*, as edited by 'Bernard Sharratt' and apparently written by several other authors, published by Harvester Press and Barnes & Noble. The declared editorial programme of this fictional periodical's was to publish reviews of books I didn't feel I had the time to write, so both the variously named reviewers and the variously authored books reviewed were wholly imaginary, but readers were cheerfully invited, if so inclined, to write the books themselves. Thirty years on, I've now revived 'NCQ' as a somewhat tongue-in-cheek vehicle for making available various writings of mine, including re-cycling some of the contents of *Literary Labyrinth*, and its companion book, *Reading Relations* (1981), which in their original very idiosyncratic forms I am happy to see remain out-of-print. So you might regard this as simply a special and belated issue of *NCQ* on Joyce.

For those perhaps interested, among the various NCQ books, *Critical Paranoia* also has something further to say about Joyce scholarship, while the short NCQ book on Yeats can be read as a companion piece to this volume. That exercise in unpacking the widening contexts for a single poem by Yeats, 'Upon a House Shaken by the Land Agitation', is concerned with the ramifications of that poem and of Coole Park, and began as an experiment in teaching Yeats in yet another post-colonial context, as a study-day for a school in Madras (Chenin) in the early 1990s. In particular, there is a deliberate shadowing of Yeats's vision of Coole Park in my focus here on 'A Boarding House' in *Dubliners*. In the spirit of the original *NCQ*, I happily leave it to others to elaborate that contrast further if they so wish.

B.S.
June 16th
2015

A warning note on Copyright

Throughout, I have quoted from my own personal copies of Joyce's works, as published in the early editions I have acquired over the years, including a Shakespeare & Co. *Ulysses* in its lovely blue paper covers, which I picked up for £40 in a condition that indicated that someone had actually read it and not just embalmed it.

I have not used or even consulted more recent critical editions since it is the Joyce who was read in his own time who primarily interests me.

As I understand the situation (see the web link below), all of Joyce's texts published during his lifetime entered the public domain as of January 1, 2012 (except perhaps in Spain). Since the first volume of his letters, a few passages from which I also quote, was published posthumously, in 1957, the copyright rule applies that in the United Kingdom works published posthumously enjoy a copyright term of only 50 years from the year of first publication. I hope.

https://joycefoundation.osu.edu/joyce-copyright/fair-use-and-permissions/about-law/public-domain

*

DUBLINERS : JOYCE'S BOARDING HOUSE

moral history

James Joyce wrote to the publisher Grant Richards on 5th May 1906:

> My intention was to write a chapter of the moral history of my country and I chose Dublin for the scene because that city seemed to me the centre of paralysis.

In 1906 Joyce was just twenty-four. He had graduated from University College, Dublin, back in 1902, and in December of that year had set off for Paris. That's roughly the point at which *A Portrait of the Artist as a Young Man* is later to leave Stephen Dedalus. In April 1903 Joyce is called back to Dublin: his mother is dying. He arrives back on Easter Sunday. But his mother takes some four months to die, finally dying on August 13th 1903. It's in the following year, 1904, that he begins writing both *Dubliners* and *Stephen Hero* (which is later to be transformed into *Portrait*).

The first *Dubliners* story appeared in *The Irish Homestead* exactly a year after his mother's death, in the issue for 13th August 1904. Two more stories appeared, 'Eveline' in September and 'After the Race' in December.

Meanwhile, in June 1904 Joyce had met Nora Barnacle. June 16th 1904 was to be become the day of *Ulysses* and Stephen Dedalus is represented in *Ulysses* as living at that time in the Martello Tower, shortly after his mother has died — though it wasn't till September 1904, a full year after his own mother's death, that Joyce himself actually lived in the tower.

In October 1904 Joyce and Nora left Dublin together, effectively for good. Over the next two years Joyce continued writing *Dubliners* stories, and *Stephen Hero*. By December 1905 twelve stories had been written, but later others were added, in particular 'The Dead', in 1907.

By 1905, however, it was clear that Joyce was going to have difficulty publishing the volume. Not only had publishers turned the collection down—that's normal, after all, for a first-time writer—but one publisher who had actually contracted to bring out the collection had raised endless objections on grounds of indecency and bad language, specifically with reference to the word 'bloody'. It was in the context of replying to some of these objections that Joyce wrote the letter I began from.

The comment that he was intending to 'write a chapter of the moral history of my country' has often been quoted as if it were self-evident, as if it were perhaps simply an anglicisation of the French term *histoire morale*, meaning something like a novel of manners or *moeurs*. But the phrase 'a chapter of the moral history' is open to at least two other and rather different readings. If one is writing a particular kind of history, a 'moral' history, then to 'write a chapter' within that history would be to provide a portion of that history which, taken together with other chapters, would constitute the wider or longer history. A chapter would describe one moment or stage within that history. This—the more obvious sense—may well have been the sense intended by Joyce.

But there is another use of the phrase 'to write a chapter', which we most often associate with battalions, regiments, and the like, which can be said to have 'written a glorious chapter' of, or in, their history. To 'write a chapter of the moral history' of one's country can perhaps carry that overtone: that the act itself constitutes an event within, and therefore itself contributes to changing, the moral history which is being unfolded.

Towards the end of the same letter we have this comment:

> Do you think that *The Second Mrs Tanqueray* would not have been denounced by a manager of the middle Victorian period, or that a publisher of that period would not have rejected a book by George Moore or Thomas Hardy? And if a change is to take place I do not see why it should not begin now.

Clearly, there is a history here: moral judgements have changed since the mid-Victorian period, and if further change is to occur, why should it not occur now. Yet, almost in the same breath, Joyce seems to argue that *Dubliners* is not, in any case, in advance of its own day. He continues:

> I do not see how the publication of *Dubliners* as it now stands in manuscript could possibly be considered an outrage on public morality.

And if *Dubliners* is not published, Joyce will be 'disappointed' but 'I do not speak so much of a material as of a moral disappointment.' Clearly, then, Joyce thinks of the publication of *Dubliners* and the reception of it as constituting a moral event.

In a later letter to Richards, on 20th May 1906, this position becomes even clearer:

> If I eliminate the points [which have been objected to] what becomes of the chapter of the moral history of my country? I fight to retain them because I believe that in composing my chapter of moral history in exactly the way I have composed it I have taken the first step towards the spiritual liberation of my country.

That seems a rather large claim for a twenty-four year old. A month later, he makes an equally extravagant claim in a final flourish to a letter in which he concedes the deletion 'of the word "bloody" wherever it occurs except in one passage in 'The Boarding House.' After that, and other concessions, he concludes:

> It is not my fault that the odour of ashpits and old weeds and offal hangs round my stories. I seriously believe that you will retard the course of civilisation in Ireland by preventing the Irish people from having one good look at themselves in my nicely polished looking-glass.

We can therefore return to that specific issue, in Joyce's further letter of 31st May 1906 to Richards. There he writes:

> You complain of Two Gallants, of a passage in Counterparts and of the word 'bloody' in Grace. Are these the only things that prevent you from publishing the book? To begin at the end: the word 'bloody' occurs in that story twice in the following passage:
>
> — At dinner, you know. Then he has a bloody big bowl of cabbage before him on the table and a bloody big spoon like a shovel etc...
>
> This I could alter, if you insist. I see no reason for doing so but if this point alone prevented the book from being published I could put another word instead of 'bloody'. But this word occurs elsewhere in the book, in Ivy Day in the Committee Room, in The Boarding House, in Two Gallants:
>
> —And one night man, she brought me two bloody fine cigars &c—
>
> Two Gallants
>
> Here's this fellow come to the throne after his bloody owl' mother keeping him out of it till the man was grey . . &c —
>
> Ivy Day in the Committee room
>
> —if any fellow tried that sort of game on with his sister he'd bloody well put his teeth down his throat, so he would &c
>
> The Boarding House
>
> The first passage I could alter. The second passage (with infinite regret) I could alter by omitting the word simply. But the third passage I absolutely could not alter. Read The Boarding House yourself and tell me frankly what you think.

> The word, the exact expression I have used, is in my opinion the one expression in the English language which can create on the reader the effect which I wish to create. Surely you can see this for yourself?

Grant Richards was an experienced publisher (he was later, incidentally, to publish Robert Tressell, even if in an abridged form). He would certainly have recognised one of the arguments that lay behind this passage. Like Joyce, he would have known the famous advice of Flaubert to Maupassant:

> Whatever you want to say, there is only one word to express it, only one verb to give it movement, only one adjective to qualify it. You must search for that word, for that verb, that adjective, and never be content with an approximation, never resort to tricks, even clever ones, and never have recourse to verbal sleight-of hand to avoid a difficulty.

That was, of course, one well-established professional creed, the 'morality of the man of letters' (to use Yeats' phrase). But for Richards the 'difficulty' involved was not aesthetic and literary but social and legal, a matter of public morality—and of potential profits. It is then important to see in what sense Joyce too was making a claim that goes beyond this Flaubertian dictum. There was a larger issue for him too.

Joyce acknowledges that he could put another word for 'bloody'. But we can ask: could the character? Think of that familiar device of censoring publishers — the dash:

> She brought me two — fine cigars

We could subsitute a variety of words here:

> She brought me two *very* fine cigars

> She brought me two *admirably* fine cigars

She brought me two *ostensibly* fine cigars

She brought me two *pretty* fine cigars

The coy dash designates an exact space to be filled by some appropriate term. And in the case of a censoring excision we actually have few doubts what the suppressed word is. But it is obviously an index of the linguistic capacity of the speaker how that gap is actually filled. Each of the terms offered above indicates a certain kind of character, with a specific verbal range and competence. But 'bloody', as a way of filling that gap is, in almost all contexts, an indication of an in-capacity, of a linguistic and cultural poverty, as not much better than a mere ellipsis. It shows an inability to find the exact word, the *mot juste*, a lazy or frustrated or irritable settling for even less than approximation, because the adequate word is beyond one's reach. But then for Joyce to provide a more adequate word where the character would have reached for 'bloody' would be to change, to falsify, that character.

To clarify what I mean by Joyce providing a more adequate term, let me give one of the rare instances where Joyce does seem to intervene with a more adequate vocabulary of his own. Compare these three passages, from the last story of all, 'The Dead':

Freddie Malins on Aunt Julia's singing:

> I was just telling my mother, he said, I never heard you sing so well, never. No, I never heard your voice so good as it is tonight. Now! Would you believe that now? That's the truth. Upon my word and honour that's the truth. I never heard your voice sound so fresh and so . . so clear and fresh, never.

Aunt Kate describing her favourite tenor, Parkinson:

> A beautiful pure sweet mellow English tenor, said Aunt Kate with enthusiasm.

And, as Bartell d'Arcy sings:

> Gabriel held up his hand for them to be silent. The song seemed to be in the old Irish tonality and the singer seemed uncertain both of his words and of his voice. The voice, made plaintive by distance and by the singer's hoarseness, faintly illuminated the cadence of the air with words expressing grief:
>
> O, the rain falls, on my heavy locks
> And the dew wets my skin,
> My babe lies cold ...

Freddie can only resort, hesitantly, to the simplest terms, repeated, recycled. Aunt Kate finds five adjectives, approaching precision. The third passage goes beyond the capacity of any of the speakers in the story: the phrase 'faintly illuminated the cadence of the air with words expressing grief' evokes and suggests yet refuses lucidity, wholly appropriately. If we could express the beauty of music in words alone we would not need music. Yet these words, exactly evocative, approach the condition of that music.

For Joyce to take us beyond the linguistic capacity of his characters is rare in these stories. His writing is normally assimilated to the speech of the Dubliners themselves, to their own linguistic range and register. And not just in the actual dialogue but in what would normally be the 'narrative voice' as well. Hugh Kenner has usefully labelled this mode or device 'The Uncle Charles Principle', taking his cue from a sentence in *Portrait*:

> Every morning, therefore uncle Charles repaired to his outhouse.

As Kenner argues, that word 'repaired' is precisely the word Uncle Charles would have used. If we are to grasp why the insistence on the word 'bloody' might eventually be justified, as a step towards the liberation of the Irish people, we should first examine in some detail how the Uncle Charles principle works. We can analyse an exemplary passage from the one story in which 'bloody' was absolutely to be retained. The passage also has a more specific aptness for our wider theme.

In the fifth paragraph of *The Boarding House* we are told that 'Mrs Mooney dealt with moral problems as a cleaver deals with meat.' A clearly inapposite mode of moral expertise, one might think. But the phrase is resonant of the environment from which Mrs Mooney herself comes; she has, after all, been married to a butcher who had gone for her with a cleaver. How the language of this story works can be suggested by a running commentary on the paragraphs which lead up to this remark, a commentary that tries to make explicit the constantly shifting voices, tones, and vocabularies of the text (what Bakhtin might call its idiolects):

> Mrs Mooney's young men paid fifteen shillings a week for board and lodgings (beer or stout at dinner excluded).

The parenthesis reads like a phrase from a clause in a contract, a qualification in a small ad., a caveat in a verbal agreement, a reminder that despite the possessive maternalism of 'Mrs Mooney's young men' her name is only a step away from 'money'.

> They shared in common tastes and occupations and for this reason they were very chummy with one another.

The unecessary pleonasm ('shared in common') and slightly arched language of social respectability clangs against the 'chummy' of a (mistaken and patronising) attempt at their own mode of speech, almost itself a failed sharing in chumminess.

> They discussed with one another the chances of favourites and outsiders.

That relatively neutral sentence comes from a speaker who is indeed an outsider to those common tastes and occupations, using 'favourites' and 'outsiders' with the fastidious detachment of one for whom they are mildly technical, even *recherché*.

> Jack Mooney, the Madam's son

The term 'Madam' ('All the resident young men spoke of her as The Madam') hovers between the respectfulness due to respectability and the dismissive vulgarity of brothel keeping.

> who was clerk to a commission agent in Fleet Street

This phrase signals, in one direction, towards a formal job description, a pretentious self-description, and in the other towards the kind of identification regularly attached to the name of the accused in a newspaper report of a minor court case.

> had the reputation of being a hard case.

No longer the deflating court-reportage but the self-preening language of the street-gang admirer.

> He was fond of using soldier's obscenities

'Fond of' almost cancels, in its approving normality, the veiled overtones of 'soldiers obscenities', itself indicating a double inadequacy of language: the soldiers themselves reduced to using obscenities, the speaker resorting to euphemism.

> usually he came home in the small hours.

The tone of an impartial anthropologist, recording nocturnal native habits, sidestepping both maternal reprimand and participant approval, flattens excess into the calming assurance of 'usually'.

> When he met his friends he had always a good one to tell them and he was always sure to be on to a good thing,

Two phrases likely to be in use among precisely such friends, but we are nevertheless given the translation:

> that is to say, a likely horse or a likely artiste.

That sly double-entendre of 'likely', linking horses and artistes, is to be echoed later. The 'translation' here is not from one formal language to another but from Jack's own discourse to a more public one, though we are soon back inside Mooney's way of speaking in:

> He was also handy with the mits and sang comic songs. On Sunday nights there would often be a reunion in Mrs Mooney's front drawing-room. The music-hall artistes would oblige . .

The female *artistes*, one is tempted to think, might indeed, in a euphemistic phrase they could perhaps use themselves, 'oblige', though in Mrs Mooney's 'front drawing-room' (to be so distinguished from her others, of course) the term so firmly attaches itself to the side of respectability as to become aristocratic in its friendly condescension, certainly a favour beyond mere commerce: *noblesse oblige.* Though Polly's song is then perhaps a trifle unfortunate in its latent truths:

> I'm a . . . naughty girl.
> You needn't sham:
> You know I am.

In the following paragraph we are more fully introduced to Polly.

> Polly was a slim girl of nineteen; she had light soft hair and a small full mouth. Her eyes, which were grey with a shade of green through them, had a habit of glancing upwards when she spoke with anyone, which made her look like a little perverse madonna.

This begins as exactly the kind of admiring self-description which Polly might want to offer of herself, but we wonder if the fine exactitude which follows (*that* shade of green) is narrative precision or preening self-congratulation. The final, devastating phrase erupts from quite elsewhere, from some bitterly *sotto voce* criticism from within her own circle (that 'little' clinches the venom).

> Mrs Mooney had first sent her daughter to be a typist in a corn-factor's office, but as a disreputable sheriff's man used to come every other day to the office . . .

Again the precison of the job-description mode, but then the scornfully dismissive and dissociating identification of the father in terms of his job seems to come both from Mrs Mooney disowning her ex-husband and from some relative stranger, perhaps an office colleague, suspicious and unknowing, unaware of the relation notified in the following phrase:

> asking to be allowed to say a word to his daughter

in which we almost hear the submissive, or sarcastic, tones of the persistent Mr Mooney himself.

> she had taken her daughter home again and set her to do housework.

A slight modification of that last phrase and cadence, to'to do *the* housework' and we would definitely hear Mrs Mooney's tone—but without the definite article, the phrase smacks rather too brutally of domestic service.

> As Polly was very lively, the intention was to give her the run of the young men.

Polly is now a filly, frisky, set loose in a paddock, a likely runner in a field of favourites and outsiders, a reasonable gamble.

Thus, by the time we come to the end of the next paragraph:

> she dealt with moral problems as a cleaver deals with meat: and in this case she had made up her mind

we have already, as readers, been faced, in a continuous fluctuation, with the task of making up our own minds as to whose language we are listening to, and whether those shifting social idiolects and colloquial registers can adequately or appropriately describe the situation.

At the same time, it is only in those very nuances and shifting tones of language themselves that we have been given the situation in the first place. We have no other access to these people, to this moral world, this ethos and environment. In a two-fold sense, the language creates them: makes them real for us and so constructs their own perceptions and experience as to render them what they are for us to know them as real at all.

I could, though at too great a length, continue through the whole story, noting the phrases resonant of a personality, a modality of morals, a tone of voice: 'She was sure she would win' . . 'she was an outraged mother' . . . 'simply abused her hospitality' . . 'a man who had seen something of the world'. . 'simply taken advantage of Polly's youth and inexperience'. . . 'must be reparation made in such a case'. . 'she counted all her cards again'.

Mrs Mooney's moral discourse is made up of these fragments of familiar reach-me-down and instant judgements, a *mélange* of theology text-book terms and sporting metaphors. When Doran himself contemplates the choice before him, and says to himself:

> she was a little vulgar; sometimes she said "I seen" and "If I had've known"

—and then asks:

> What would grammar matter if he really loved her?

—there is a sense in which he formulates in the specific case, but too literally, the general problem before us: whether we think love is possible without an adequate grammar for it, whether we consider morality to be possible without an adequate syntax and vocabulary for moral discourse.

The more general issue for the reader in both these stories — and in all the *Dubliners* stories, though in different ways — is that the language deployed by the story itself maps onto and almost perfectly matches the language of the characters within the story: Kenner's 'Uncle Charles principle' at work. So if we are to demand a more adequate response, in a more adequate language, we will have to provide it ourselves.

moral language

Joyce does not, however, leave us entirely alone in this task. In the significant revisions he made to the opening story (in May and June 1906, in the same months as his correspondence with Richards) we are given some terms for at least grasping the problem itself. We are given an appropriate technical term for that concluding moment in'Counterparts' we will look at later, that pitiful attempt to utilise a religious practice as part of a contractual exchange — at its simplest, the selling of spiritual power, or religious knowledge, for money or other benefits. The proper theological term for this is 'simony', one of the three words which the young boy in 'The Sisters'' says softly to himself:

> Every night as I gazed up at the window I said softly to myself the word paralysis. It had always sounded strangely in my ears, like the word gnomon in the Euclid and the word simony in the Catechism.

The two text-books, of mathematical and moral-religious education, the *Euclid* and the *Catechism*, provide two of the words, while perhaps a third, the surreptitiously consulted medical text-book, provides a partial grasp of the third term: not just physical immobility but General Paralysis of the Insane (GPI), endemic disease of a syphillitically corrupted Dublin.

In what was to have been the original conclusion in the sequence of stories, the end of 'Grace'', we again have the evocation of simony in the form of a financial metaphor for one's spiritual relationship with God. The priest, in the sermon directed to businessmen, reaches for the language of accounting in his summing up:

> But one thing only, he said, he would ask of his hearers. And that was: to be straight and manly with God. If their accounts tallied in every point to say: 'Well, I have verified my accounts. I find all well.' But if, as might happen, there were some discrepancies, to admit the truth, to be frank and say like a man: 'Well, I have looked into my accounts. I find this wrong and this wrong. But, with God's grace, I will rectify this and this. I will set right my accounts.'

To think of one's relationship with God according to the model of double-entry book-keeping may well have a certain respectable history: that great contemporary sociologist, Max Weber, had already drawn attention to the intimate linking of capitalism and the rise of protestantism. But for the Catholic-minded Joyce, if not for the Catholic priest, this language is surely to be judged as inadequate and inappropriate.

But it is not the only or the worst form of linguistic inadequacy or inappropriateness. In that first story again, as the relatives and neighbours assemble to mourn the death of the priest, they arrange themselves in a moment of familiar domestic ritual. They take their seats, a little glass of sherry and some cream crackers (socially refined sacramental substitutes?) are offered, and declined. Then:

> No one spoke: we all gazed at the empty fireplace.
>
> My aunt waited until Eliza sighed and then said:
> 'Ah, well, he's gone to a better world.'
> Eliza sighed again and bowed her head in assent. My aunt fingered the stem of her wine-glass before sipping a little.
> 'Did he . . . peacefully?' she asked.
> 'Oh, quite peacefully, ma'am,' said Eliza. 'You couldn't tell when the breath went out of him. He had a beautiful death, God be praised.'
> 'And everything . . . ?'
> 'Father O'Rourke was in with him a Tuesday and anointed him and prepared him and all.'
> 'He knew then?'

> 'He was quite resigned.'
> 'He looks quite resigned,' said my aunt.
> 'That's just what the woman we had in to wash him said. She said he just looked as if he was asleep, he looked that peaceful and resigned. No one would think he'd make such a beautiful corpse.'
> 'Yes, indeed,' said my aunt.

Said in a certain tone and accent, with suitable poised pauses, this bout of what the sociolinguists call 'sympathetic circularity' could almost be a hilariously parodic comic routine on the banality of speech, an ideal script for a comedy duo (perhaps Peter Cook and Dudley Moore). Each dotted ellipsis can evoke that desperately polite in-capacity to say anything meaningful at all which characterises so many social situations for the refined English-speaking classes. The giggles are just an intake of breath away.

This moment of embarrassed absence of appropriate words is itself echoed on the penultimate page of the complete sequence of stories, when Gabriel Conroy anticipates another family funeral:

> Soon, perhaps, he would be sitting in that same drawing-room, dressed in black, his silk hat on his knees. The blinds would be drawn down and Aunt Kate would be sitting beside him, crying and blowing her nose and telling him how Julia had died. He would cast about in his mind for some words that might console her, and would find only lame and useless ones. Yes, yes: that would happen very soon.

There is something desperately beyond irony in the notion that the family of a Catholic priest, confronted with his death, should have no words in which to articulate their response to that death. For if the christian understanding of death should transform that occasion into an opportunity for celebration, in the hope of the resurrection, then this flat, low-key, mono-dimensional absence of language surely constitutes in itself an indictment of a religious culture which so disables its adherents.

A pagan wake would be preferable. But in the very first sentence of the book we have already been told: 'There was no hope for him. ' If there is no hope within that christian faith, no hope of the resurrection, then perhaps that cultural-religious frame of feeling and belief has simply become empty and hollow. Even when your own mother dies.

gnomon

There are two other moments within that opening story when the possibility of an adequate language is directly broached. One is when the boy attempts to pray at the bedside and finds he cannot. The other comes in the second paragraph:

> Old Cotter was sitting at the fire, smoking, when I came downstairs to supper. While my aunt was ladling out my stirabout he said, as if returning to some former remark of his:
> 'No, I wouldn't say he was exactly . . . but there was something queer . . . there was something uncanny about him. I'll tell you my opinion . . . '
> He began to puff at his pipe, no doubt arranging his opinion in his mind. Tiresome old fool! When we knew him first he used to be rather interesting, talking of faints and worms; but I soon grew tired of him and his endless stories about the distillery.
> 'I have my own theory about it, " he said. 'I think it was one of those . . . peculiar cases . . . But it's hard to say . . . '

Those dots across the page are again eloquent of an absence, an emptiness. The sympathetic circularity that can normally be relied upon to assume the correct response can easily falter here, since it is wholly unclear just what Cotter's incomplete contributions are to be. The words are not so much left hanging as simply throttled at birth. Perhaps we do not even have the words for that kind of emptiness and absence, that gap. And perhaps the speakers do not even know that they do not have them or need them.

In talking of faints and worms Old Cotter was employing a technical vocabulary, of brewing, that seemed at first every-day ordinary language. Similarly misleading is perhaps the word 'paralysis'. However, here the third highlighted term of that opening paragraph, 'gnomon', begins to suggest its role. It clearly signals itelf as undeniably extra-ordinary, a word that we don't normally have to hand, demanding dictionary consultation.

Three senses of 'gnomon' hover: the spike on a sundial; the geometrical sense; and a possible third, related to the 'gnome' (cf. gnomic) which as a form of writing used to include the 'sceal' form, a kind of aphorism which was able to carry simultaneously the two senses, that 'good men ought to do X' and that 'good men characteristically do X.' In this usage, a 'gnome' hovers across and combines what we would distinguish as the prescriptive and the descriptive, those same divisions between an older 'moral' inquiry and the new 'science of moral facts'. Arguably perhaps, Joyce's own mode of writing is to reveal itself as simultaneously descriptive and implicitly prescriptive.

But it is the geometric sense, the Euclid sense, which is uppermost. The term originally denoted a carpenter's square, the right-angle ruler of the traditional craft. It came to refer to that part of a parallelogram which remains when a section exactly congruent in shape to the whole parallelogram is removed from it (giving, with a right-angle parallelogram, the carpenter's set-square of the etymology). What we then have is a hole with the same shape as the whole.

In *Dubliners* we seem to have a morality-shaped hole, an emptiness which itself indicates the whole-ness which is unavailable. We might even think of a sentence with a censoring dash or an ellipsis of inadequacy in it, one which could only be filled appropriately by the sentence itself, once rendered complete. It is this sense of gnomon which, finally, is crucial to Joyce's assumed project of writing a chapter of moral history. We can begin to see why by considering a hypothesis, a speculative interpretation of a moment in Joyce's life already referred to.

Consider yourself returning from Paris, to arrive on Easter Sunday to see a dying mother. But she does not die till four months later. Throughout that time, there is ample opportunity to reflect on one insistent fact: that nothing in one's given faith or culture can adequately account for, explain, make sense of, console one for, allow one to come to terms with, provide a language for, this death, this dying. There is no language for the death of a mother. We know that when we gather at the death-bed or the funeral or the grave-side the only words we will have available will be inadequate and yet they will be the only ones.

Even to call them inadequate is inadequate. Whether the family sit in sympathetic silence, or speak in flatly elliptical phrases, broken not by grief but by emptiness, that is the truth of the situation. It is not some substitute for a more adequate language of death. There is no language of death. Only, if it were true, a language of hope beyond, and after, and against death. A language of resurrection. The language of Easter Sunday. But for Joyce this cannot be the true language.

Again, the letter to Nora, 29th August 1904, a fortnight after the first anniversary of the death:

> When I looked upon her face as she lay in her coffin—a face grey and wasted with cancer—I understood that I was looking on the face of a victim and I cursed the sytem that had made her a victim. We were seventeen in family. My brothers and sisters are nothing to me. One brother alone is capable of understanding me.
>
> Six years ago I left the Catholic church, hating it most fervently.

Sending Nora his first published story, as it appeared on the very day of the first anniversary itself, Joyce writes to her, perhaps ambiguously:

> I believe there was hardly a thought in my head all day but one.

Perhaps the only adequate response to death is love, substitution, the Oedipal resolution of finding a new love.

The *Dubliners* stories will be haunted by death, as the rest of Joyce's *oeuvre* will be shaped by death: the priest will die in 'The Sisters'; another in 'Araby'; a mother has died in ''Eveline'; Maria will choose the clay; Mrs Sinico's death will be reported; Parnell's death will be remembered; Gabriel will feel himself approaching the vast region of the dead. *Dubliners* ends with 'The Dead', *Portrait* ends with Stephen's trip to Paris, his clothes packed by his mother, soon to be dead (though Joyce did return, once, between the departure and the inadequate paternal telegram: 'Come home. Mother dying').

Ulysses will begin from the insult of that mother being "beastly dead"—not an insult to his mother but an insult to Stephen, since a dead beast can no longer be insulted. But is a dead mother simply a now-decaying animal? Or can her spirit walk? *Finnegans Wake* will revolve round the waking of the dead, in all senses of the words. And the dead are, after all, what history is. History is the dead. As I write this, today is the anniversary of Joyce's mother's death, August 13th. Who now remembers that?

Joyce made good use of that death in his art. Even a mother's death can be the subject matter of art. Faced with that crushing gap and absence, and the inadequacies of language at the heart of his experience and of his culture, Joyce managed to wrest from it the task of creating a new conscience, a new consciousness. But as artist, not as the priest his mother might once have hoped for. And that, of course, was the difficulty, the substantial task. Dublin had a place for its priests and even its poets, and above all for its story-tellers, especially its tellers of tales about the glorious dead. But if Joyce were simply to tell Dublin its own stories, his looking glass would not be that of an artist. Again, the letter to Stanislaus, 19th July 1905:

> I saw the extreme putridity of the social system out of which Goldsmith had reared his flower. Is it possible that, after all, men of letters are no more than entertainers? . . .

> The stories in *Dubliners* seem to be indisputably well done but, after all, perhaps many people could do them as well. . . The Dublin papers will object to my stories as to a caricature of Dublin life. Do you think there is any truth in this?

How Joyce, who was after all a Dubliner, came to be the Dubliner who could write *Dubliners* was perhaps a matter for *A Portrait.* But first we have to consider why the *Dubliners* stories are not, after all, simply stories of Dubliners.

In Joyce's case there is, moreover, another kind of judgement involved, another context, that of literature and its adequacy or otherwise. The fuller context for the excerpt above deserves consideration:

> The preface to *The Vicar of Wakefield* which I read yesterday gave me a moment of doubt as to the excellence of my literary manners. It seems so improbable that Hardy, for example, will be spoken of in two hundred years. And yet when I arrived at page two of the narrative I saw the extreme putridity of the social system out of which Goldsmith had reared his flower. Is it possible that, after all, men of letters are no more than entertainers? These discouraging reflections arise perhaps from my surroundings. The stories in *Dubliners* seem to be indisputably well done but, after all, perhaps many people could do them as well. I am not rewarded by any feeling of having overcome difficulties. Maupassant writes very well, of course, but I am afraid that his moral sense is rather obtuse. . . Of course do not think that I consider contemporary Irish writing anything but ill-written, morally obtuse formless caricature.

For Joyce there is clearly a connection, even though Maupassant's case questions it, between the quality of writing and the quality of moral judgement, between formlessness and moral obtuseness.

And there are further links between the putrid social system which he repudiates, his own moral impulses which he endorses, as against the commerical and contract-minded notions of moral duty, and his capacity for writing as no-one else could have — even though precisely that capacity might involve him in contractual difficulties with publishers and general moral obloquy.

For it can indeed seem that it is not only the characters' own language, vocabulary, tone, idiom and clichés that we are given. The stories too seem to be the kinds of story these characters would tell themselves. In Dublin, it is clear, stories circulate; the life of Dublin is almost as made up of stories as is *Dubliners* itself.

The children in 'An Encounter' read and en-act Wild West stories; Eveline listens to (presumably tall?) stories from Frank, and one of her more poignant memories is of that one occasion when her father read her a ghost story; in 'A Little Cloud', Gallagher tells (presumably tall?) stories, and Little Chandler imagines versions of them featuring himself; in 'Counterparts' Farrington retells, indeed retails, the story of the *riposte* to the boss several times over in several pubs (as the narrator of Cyclops will tell and re-tell the story of Bloom and the Citizen); at the end of 'A Boarding House' Polly will be so absorbed in the day-dreaming stories she tells herself about her own future that she forgets why she is dreaming them. Old Cotter tells his stories of the distillery till boredom prevails; Parnell's successors tell stories of petty politicians: a horse goes round and round a statue and the story of the horse goes round and round Dublin.

Each of these stories, then, could simply be told by a Dubliner. But a difference emerges as soon as each is taken within the specific context given by all the other stories in *Dubliners*. Joyce's letter to Richards of 5th May 1906 had continued:

> I chose Dublin for the scene because that city seemed to me the centre of paralysis. I have tried to present it to the indifferent public under four of its aspects: childhood, adolescence, maturity and public life. The stories are arranged in this order. I have written it for the most part in

a style of scrupulous meanness and with the conviction that he is a very bold man who dares to alter in the presentment, still more to deform, what he has seen and heard.
I cannot do any more than this.

The 'four aspects' provide one way of taking the collection as systematically organised, as a whole, with a shape. But there are several other layers of insinuated systematicity. The stories are often linked by patterning devices, by for example the use of compass points (Wild West, exotic East, North Wall, South America) or the motif of light (Chandler, candles, power stations).

Secondly, there is a strong sense that incidents in one story form, as it were, the off-screen space for other stories. A priest can die in one house, and a house in another story can be named as that in which a priest once died. A pub can be the meeting-place of one set of characters, while another walks past an unnamed pub. Two boys can make their way to the docks, while a girl stands fixed at the dock gates.

Thirdly, it often seems that the individuals within each story, as we move through those various stages of life Joyce outlined, might re-figure at some later stage in their own life-cycle in some of the other stories, or untold variations of them. The boy who unexpectedly is to become a priest in 'An Encounter' might later give a retreat sermon to businessmen; Corley might some day become the kind of lonely pervert encountered in that same story; Eveline may end up as the skivvy of 'Two Gallants' or perhaps as another Maria; Gabriel Conroy might have been a Gallagher, or a Mr Duffy. But not a Joyce.

This aspect of the collection has the important effect that insofar as we tend to identify initially with the children in the opening stories (it is from their outlook that we seem to read, albeit already as adults), and we are also aware that those children might well turn out to be the unprepossessing protagonists of the later stories, we too can see ourselves as potentially liable to become versions of those later figures. We can therefore tend towards seeing them as victims of a putrid social system, rather than simply as morally responsible or irresponsible.

A fourth way in which a certain systematicity is suggested within *Dubliners* is by our awareness that the absence in any particular case of an adequate moral vocabulary, response or insight, is itself an instance of a wider inadequacy, a case of general paralysis, a general inadequacy of all the social languages available, a syphillitic infection of language..

To grasp the nature of systematicity could itself constitute a change in moral history: to see a society as a 'system', over and above the individuals who comprise it. Precisely that awareness seems to have registered powerfully with Joyce at his mother's death. But to recognise the workings of a 'system' means that one might then refuse both moral blame and special pleading, the excuse of exceptional conditions.

The overall form of *Dubliners*, neither single novel nor simple collection, means that no single protagonist becomes a centre for special pleading, the focus of our attention and sympathy. All privileged positions are undermined, even that of the narrative voice itself. Every protagonist becomes a focus and yet each protagonist is relativised in relation to all those other Dubliners.

Consider now the nicely titled 'Counterparts'. It's clear that Farrington is indeed a bully and brutally obtuse, but it's also clear that Farrington is himself only one link in a chain of brutality, of the exercise of power and force. Yet that power is not exercised by some impersonal category over and above Farrington: he remains the agent of his own bullying. The 'system' is not simply external; each is the condition of another. *Dubliners* delineates the interaction of Dubliners upon each other, even though that interaction is not fully shown, is left largely off-screen. In the development of sociology this deep logic of society was acknowledged: society, precisely as constituted by people, has its own logic.

Joyce's indicative term for this is paralysis: GPI, syphillis, can be seen as a condition of an entire social existence; the disease becomes a social disease through the actions of individuals upon and with one another, yet those actions are in one sense inescapable for the society to exist at all. Once the disease is endemic our actions, whether we intend it or not, contribute to the furtherance of the disease.

We can now recognise this most acutely in the spread of AIDS but William Blake had already seen it in the charted streets of London where

> the harlot's curse
> Blasts the new born infant's tear
> And blights with plague the marriage hearse.

Once the recognition of the logic of the social (socio-logy) has emerged, it is possible to see that one's contribution to changing that system can include changing oneself, since one is also a condition, not only a product, of that system. Even though one might be a Dubliner, the conditions under which one can cease to be simply paralysed rest to some extent within one's own grasp. But the first step is to see oneself as victim, as caught in the nets, to see oneself as already history.

Reflexivity is thus the first step. But that requires language and language too is a system, and—crucially—it is indeed constituted by what we actually speak, not as some powerful but inert externality. Therefore one's own language can be, or perhaps has to be, worked upon, revised, transformed.And that occurs by microscopic effort, close attention, detailed amendment, taking what one says and writes just a shade away from the language that has been inherited, towards the one word that will do the exact job required. That is the beginning of an awareness that language, and perhaps what we call society, can perhaps be radically modified. It's the first step towards *Finnegans Wake.* It is the crucial step for the literary artist.

mot juste

We can draw our various contexts and commentaries together. For Joyce to become an artist was a chapter in his own moral history, and perhaps a crucial moment in that history was his reaction to his mother's death. But in transforming what he had seen and heard in Dublin into *Dubliners* Joyce was transmuting the materials of a sociology into literature, the distinction lying precisely in the insistence upon the very language of *Dubliners* as the substantial material of a moral history: not etymology, as Nietzsche had suggested, but the range and register of actual current language, the languages of uncle Charles and aunt Kate.

But in recording and presenting those languages Joyce presented also their gaps, hesitancies, absences, silences, inadequacies— and thereby the need for an art that would transform the language itself. The paradoxical *gnomon* of *Dubliners* is a shape which includes a missing shape which when presented as missing would refigure the whole and complete it. But if art was needed to show this, that art required an artist.

For Joyce to become that artist was then not only a chapter in his own history but a contribution to the spiritual liberation of his people. For if he could so change himself, any Dubliner might also do so. In particular, even a Catholic Dubliner from a bizarre sociological combination of urban slum and university education, could show that the aristocratic haven of Coole Park, that more sophisticated boarding house for artistes, was no longer necessary for the commitments and perfections of art. That chapter was already closed.

The final paragraph of *Dubliners*, the closing of 'he Dead', with its evocation of a Galway churchyard not too far from Coole, and its awareness of snow falling all over Ireland, is perhaps the moment at which Joyce finally declares himself and speaks in the language of his own art. If Irish faith and culture provided no language for death and dying, Joyce had finally done so. He had served his apprenticeship.

Here is Ezra Pound, reviewing Joyce's *Portrait*, in February 1917:

> If more people had read *The Portrait* and certain stories in Mr Joyce's *Dubliners* there might have been less recent trouble in Ireland. A clear diagnosis is never without its value. . . It is very important that there should be clear, unexaggerated, realistic literature. It is very important that there should be good prose. The hell of contemporary Europe is caused by the lack of representative government in Germany, and by the non-existence of decent prose in the German language. Clear thought and sanity depend on clear prose. . . A nation that cannot write clearly cannot be trusted to govern, nor yet to think.

For Pound, writing a year after the Easter rising, Joyce's style is almost an index of whether Ireland is yet ready for self-government. In *How to Read* Pound was to ask: 'Has literature a function in the state?' And to answer:

> It has to do with the clarity and vigour of 'any and every' thought and opinion. It has to do with maintaining the very cleanliness of the tools, the health of the very matter of thought itself. . .the individual cannot think and communicate his thought, the governor and legislator cannot act effectively or frame his laws, without words, and the solidity and validity of these words is in the care of the damned and despised litterati. When their work goes rotten —by that I do not mean when they express indecorous thoughts —but when their very medium, the very essence of their work, their application of word to thing goes rotten, i.e. becomes slushy and inexact, or excessive or bloated, the whole machinery of social and of individual thought and order goes to pot. This is a lesson of history, and a lesson not yet half learned.

Possibly a lesson from that moral history in which Joyce's work was to be a chapter. Finally, in his review of *Ulysses* , Pound explicitly aligns the gifts of the writer with 'the gifts that govern men' (though not quite in that exact phrase of Yeats) and registers a clear riposte to any lingering aesthetes on precisely the issue raised in Wilde's Preface to *Dorian Gray* (another portrait):

> A Fabian milk report is of less use to a legislator than the knowledge contained in *L'Education Sentimentale*, or in *Bovary*. The legislator is supposed to manage human affairs, to arrange for comity of human agglomerations. *Le beau monde gouverne*—or did once—because it had access to condensed knowledge, the middle ages were ruled by those who could read, an aristocracy received Macchiavelli's treatise before the serfs. . . The *mot juste* is of public utility. I can't help it. I am not offering this fact as a sop to aesthetes who want all authors to be fundamentally useless.

> We are governed by words, the laws are graven in words, and literature is the sole means of keeping these words living and accurate.

In echoing Wilde here, Pound was perhaps forgetting that Wilde had, after all, come to know that even a Preface declaring the uselessness of art might itself prove useful to legislators—in helping to secure a conviction for immorality. Later, of course, Pound faced his own possible conviction for his own choice of language and of allegiance.

a sociology of morality

Developing from the 1890s, in the work of Emile Durkheim, above all, yet another context can be found for an attempt to write a 'moral history' connecting city and morality. In that brief period when Joyce had first been in Paris, in 1902-3, Professor Durkheim, the newly appointed luminary at the Sorbonne, had been giving his famous lectures on 'Moral Education'. In 1903 Levy-Bruhl had published his controversial, even provocative, *La Morale et la science des moeurs*, quickly translated into English in 1905 as *Ethics and Moral Science.* And in 1902 Durkheim's crucial work, *The Division of Labour in Society*, first published in 1893, had been given an important second edition.

The shared project and programme of these founding texts of sociology was the study of 'morality' scientifically, objectively, not as a normative discipline but as a 'positive science of moral facts' (to quote Durkheim reviewing Levy-Bruhl). Durkheim in particular had argued that Europe was in the midst of a moral crisis, or a crisis of morality, as the full impact of the shift from traditional rural ways of living to the new urban environment was felt. In that new situation, there was a need to create a new common '*conscience*' (in French, both consciousness and conscience), and the initial contribution had to be that of the 'rational moral art'of sociology, that of studying and presenting what the actual moral behaviour of people really was.

As a crucial element in this project, the division between country and city had itself been given a new history. In Durkheim's *Division of Labour* we are offered a brief account of the transition from agricultural to urban social organisation, as the context within which certain crucial changes of the present day are to be understood. Durkheim writes:

> As we advance in the evolutionary scale, the ties which bind the individual to his family, to his native soil, to traditions which the past has given him, to collective group usages, become loose. More mobile, he changes his environment more easily, leaves his people to go elsewhere to live a more autonomous existence, to a greater extent forms his own ideas and sentiments. Of course, the whole common conscience does not, on this account, pass out of existence.

I would be intrigued to know if the Joyce who had left for Paris in an exile chosen both in order to live a more autonomous existence and, perhaps, to forge a common conscience for his race, ever read or heard, in those crucial months, this highly fashionable French sociologist. Durkheim again:

> We can say that in higher societies, our duty is not to spread our activity over a large surface [the agricultural mode] but to concentrate and specialize it [the urban mode]. We must contract our horizon, choose a definite task and immerse ourselves in it completely, instead of trying to make ourselves a sort of creative masterpiece, quite complete, which contains its worth in itself and not in the services that it renders.

Again, one is tempted to contrast the Wilde who had nothing to declare but his genius with the Joyce who was to calculate the precise number of man-hours spent on every work.

Durkheim concludes his whole book:

> It has been said with justice that morality—and by that must be understood not only moral doctrines but customs

> — is going through a real crisis. . . Profound changes have been produced in the structure of our societies in a very short time; . . accordingly the morality which corresponds to this social type has regressed, but without another developing quickly enough to fill the ground that the first left vacant in our consciences. . . Because certain of our duties are no longer founded in the reality of things, a breakdown has resulted which will be repaired only insofar as a new discipline is established and consolidated. In short, our first duty is to make a moral code for ourselves.

One can think here of Joyce's first essayistic version of 'Portrait of the Artist', with its emphasis upon personal and individual self-realisation, of establishing one's own conscience and moral nature. At that point, Durkheim would perhaps link hands with the Wilde of *The Soul of Man Under Socialism*, with its argument that only socialism would enable true individualism. In 1909 Joyce published an article on Wilde, and wrote to Wilde's literary executor, seeking permission to translate *Soul of Man under Socialism* into Italian.

There is clearly some affinity between Joyce's scrupulous meanness, the realist descriptive exactitude in *Dubliners* and some of the methodological and investigative techniques which accompanied the rise of empirical sociology. Joyce's choice of Dublin as the focus for his moral history might even be placed alongside such contemporary efforts as those of Charles Booth, whose *Life and Labour In London* was finally completed in 1903. Though it is also worth recalling that 'The Sisters' first appeared in *The Irish Homestead*, on 13th August 1904, tucked away amid the adverts for agricultural machinery.

moral history

The final context into which one might place Joyce's remark is the history of moral thinking. Durkheim had argued that moral thought itself had entered into crisis at the turn of the century. Though he denied that the intellectual crisis was the cause of any wider moral malaise, that crisis had registered in the intellectual debate about 'morals'.

In the long development of the dual heritage from Kant and Hegel—one taken as asserting the inescapable givenness of moral duty, the inexorability of the moral imperative, the other regarded as laying the foundations for a relativisation of all morality within a history of consciousness—the high point of crisis seemed to have been reached with Nietzsche's *Genealogy of Morals*. In the Preface, dated 1887, Nietzsche anticipated what Durkheim was to propose, a historical sociology of morality:

> We need a critique of all moral values; the intrinsic worth of these values must, first of all, be called in question. To this end we need to know the conditions from which those values have sprung, and how they have developed and changed: morality as consequence, symptom, mask, *tartufferie*, sickness, misunderstanding; but, also, morality as cause, remedy, stimulant, inhibition, poison. . . The object is to explore the huge, distant and thoroughly hidden country of morality, morality as it has actually existed and actually been lived

—though Nietzsche here warns against any mere 'random hypothesising in the English manner'. Joyce was perhaps to remember Nietzsche's own speculative account of the transition from nobility to mediocrity (Nietzsche's variation of the move from epic to novel, from country to urbanity) in terms of the Gaelic word:

> *fin*, as in Fingal, the characteristic term for nobility, eventually the good, noble, pure, originally the fair-haired as opposed to the dark, black haired native population.

However, despite Nietzsche's disdain, even the Anglo-Saxon intellectual world had already seen, in the work of the Hegelian philosopher F. H. Bradley, an early formulation of that symptomatically self-cancelling 20th-century question: 'Why should I be moral? ' (Bradley, *Ethical Studies*, 1876, essay 2). Bradley had analysed the predictable 19th century response in his essay on 'My station and its duties'.

By 1903, with the publication of G. E. Moore's *Principia Ethica,* the more fashionable appeal was to an intuitive, ungrounded moral sense. But even in England historical sociology was intruding: in 1906 Westermarck published his *The Origin and Development of the Moral Ideas*—though, as Durkheim sadly pointed out, this ostensible attempt to 'study moral facts scientifically' remained trapped in the search for 'fundamental, universal tendencies' without relating the differences 'between the various forms each moral rule assumes' to 'the social milieu from which it issues. '

Nietzsche had once suggested a crucial question to be tackled: 'What light does the science of linguistics, especially the study of etymology, throw on the evolution of moral ideas?' Eventually, one persuasive analysis of 'moral history' would combine the philosopher's questions, the historian's inquiries, and the etymologist's insights, to recast and reinterpret Durkheim's mapping of the transition from agricultural to urban existence, from heroic battle to commercial enterprise, from warrior tribe to bourgeois respectability.

Alasdair MacIntyre, in his various works on the history of ethics and morality, traces three symptomatic stages in which the verb 'own' moves to the verb 'ought'. In the first stage, 'own' indicates the ownership of possession, of power as the basis of conquest and right; in this social formation duties and obligations are given by status allocation, by feudal role, by pre-given place in the social structure.

In a second stage, the word 'own' slides into the commercial, contractual obligation of 'owe' premissed, as Hume pointed out, on a form of social fiction, that of the binding promise; here obligations are a matter of contract, even conceptualised as a 'social contract' of free individuals.

But this yields to a third stage, to a detachable sense of 'ought', of obligation over and above the contractual or legal requirement: what emerges is a specifically ethical sense of obligation.

This final sense is often entwined with a converging development in religious sensibility, in which the God of power and awe, of arbitrary fate and destiny, is replaced first by a God of Covenant, of promise, of loyalty to a community, and then, as a curious and perhaps unstable fusion of impersonal demand and personal exemplar of moral rectitude, into a God of whom it could indeed be asked why he seemed unable to live up to his own moral demands, to his own divine station and its duties.

It is, intriguingly, possible to identify all three of these stages in one complex moment in *Dubliners*, at the end of 'Counterparts'. The threatened child tries to ward off his father's blows:

> 'O, pa! ' he cried. 'Don't beat me, pa! And I'll . . I'll say a Hail Mary for you . . I'll say a Hail Mary for you, pa, if you don't beat me . . I'll say a Hail Mary . . . '

In that single moment, we have the three stages in the history of morality. First, the power and physical punishment, the injustice of mere brute strength of arm, giving 'rights' over others, based upon kin and sheer physical control.

Then, second, the child attempts to mitigate the effects of that arbitrary force by offering a contract and a promise: 'don't beat me . . and I'll say a Hail Mary'. But, third, and incorporated within the contractual promise, the offered exchange and transaction, is a practice, that of petitionary prayer, taken directly from that allegedly superior stage, the ethical-religious. But, of course, in utilising prayer as a bargaining factor in the pathetic and impotent currency of the oppressed, the boy is both reducing religion to commerce and regressing to the most primitive stage of all: fear as the basis of morals.

If we were to treat Joyce's 'moral history' as making a 'genuine contribution to the sociological study of Irish affairs' we could indeed take his account of father-son relations here as evidence and starting point for a quite far-reaching analysis, and arrive— the more we probed it—at a profoundly plausible historical account. All three stages of morality could be shown as still in play in Joyce's Dublin and, as good sociologists, we could easily relate them to differential stages in the history of that city.

Clearly, then, we can envisage several overlapping contexts for Joyce's claim to be writing 'a chapter of the moral history of my country'. And once we place his claim alongside these more or less contemporary and cognate efforts, of sociologists and philosophers, the phrase can take on a more precise and intelligible meaning. Nevertheless, the extravagance of the claim surely remains. Joyce, after all, was not in fact offering an empirically based sociological inquiry, but a fiction. Moreover, his specific claim, in its immediate context, seems to rest upon an implausible premise. Publishing a multi-volume study of London labour, or a major theoretical treatise in sociological method. might be a crucial contribution, but surely it was a wholly inflated claim to argue that the publication of the word 'bloody' in a short story would somehow constitute the first step in the spiritual liberation of Ireland.

Or, on second thoughts, perhaps not so inflated a claim.

*

Does Stephen Dedalus become an artist? On the logic that emerges for us in *Dubliners* the crucial evidence would lie in his language. In *Portrait* we can read at least some of Stephen's writings, especially his Journal. The first entry:

> March 20. Long talk with Cranly on the subject of my revolt. He had his grand manner on. I supple and suave. Attacked me on the score of love for one's mother. Tried to imagine his mother: cannot. Told me once, in a moment of thoughtlessness, his father was sixty-one when he was born. Can see him. Strong farmer type. Pepper and salt suit. Square feet. Unkempt, grizzled beard. Probably attends coursing matches. Pays his dues regularly but not plentifully to Father Dwyer of Larras. Sometimes talks to girls after nightfall. But his mother? Very young or very old? Hardly the first. If so, Cranly would not have spoken as he did. Old then. Probably, and neglected. Hence Cranly's despair of soul: the child of exhausted loins.

There might be several judgements of this. We have some evidence for how accurate, or honest, a self-description the adjectives 'supple and suave' are, since we have a version of that conversation to compare it with. But we have no other access to Cranly's parents than Stephen has. And here Stephen's imagination seems not only unable to imagine a mother but incapable of imagining more than a father composed of clichés, a predictable set of characteristics, a thin imagining. What seems in play here is an imagination without the kind of sympathetic insight into other human beings which has been regarded as the pre-requisite for one kind of claim to be an artist: that maturity and fullness of human response to others which can be claimed as both the qualification and the contribution of the writer. Stephen's imagination seems lacking in such sympathy or insight.

We can compare it with Cranly's own attention to others, in the conversation referred to. We might also ask if Cranly here has 'his grand manner on':

> Let me ask you a question. Do you love your mother?
> Stephen shook his head slowly.
> I don't know what your words mean, he said simply.
> Have you ever loved anyone? Cranly asked.
> Do you mean women?
> I am not speaking of that, Cranly said in a colder tone. I ask if you ever felt love towards anyone or anything?
> Stephen walked on beside his friend, staring gloomily at the footpath.
> I tried to love God, he said at length. It seems now I failed. It is very difficult. I tried to unite my will with the will of God instant by instant. In that I did not always fail. I could perhaps do that still
> Cranly cut him short by asking:
> Has your mother had a happy life?
> How do I know? Stephen said.
> How many children had she?
> Nine or ten, Stephen answered. Some died.

A few more precise questions and Cranly is shortly able to conclude that Stephen's mother must have gone through a great deal of suffering.

It's a difference of method, of tone, and of character. It would be possible to argue that without both the capacity for love which Cranly sees as missing and something of Cranly's own sympathetic identification, Stephen will never be an artist. An artist, so the familiar argument would run, needs to create characters who convince us and with whom we can sympathise and even identify. As Joyce had done with Stephen's own character.

There is, however, a quite other mode of writing. As in the second diary entry:

> March 21, morning. Thought this in bed last night but was too lazy and free to add to it. Free, yes. The exhausted loins are those of Elizabeth and Zachary. Then he is the precursor. Item: he eats chiefly belly bacon and dried figs. Read locusts and wild honey. Also, when thinking of him, saw always a stern severed head or death mask as if outlined on a grey curtain or veronica.

> Decollation they call it in the gold. Puzzled for the moment by saint John at the Latin gate. What do I see? A decollated precursor trying to pick the lock.

The imagination here is not working upon believable characterisation, but upon patterns and resonances, allegories and correspondences. It is perhaps an older mode of literary creation than the realist-humanist tradition of the novel. The text turns self-consciously upon itself and upon its reader, who has to recall at least two other passages:

> Cranly dislodged a figseed from his teeth on the point of his rude toothpick and gazed at it intently.

If the reader has not already paused and thought intently about this passage at the time, the suggested interpretation in the diary will be both an illumination and a rebuke. The invitation to unpick the lock was there all the time. We had also been given the clue about the beheading:

> Why was it that when he thought of Cranly he could never raise before his mind the entire image of his body but only the image of the head and face? Even now against the grey curtain of the morning he saw it before him like the phantom of a dream, the face of a severed head or death mask . . .

We should, it seems, as readers, have tried to answer that 'Why?' for ourselves. And now, reading the diary entry, we are invited to pause and ponder the fuller significances of Saint John, of severed heads, and of the Veronica. And: 'Free, yes.' That is addressed to an accomplice reader, *frère lecteur*. And if Stephen is able to grasp these correspondences and elaborate them so confidently, perhaps he has the makings of a quite different kind of artist, and will become one without the need for love or sympathetic imagination.

Our question as to whether Stephen becomes an artist thus remains open, if only because two rather different notions of artist come into play in these two passages. But of course it is not simply the ending of the novel which is ambivalent. Rather, there are two distinct ways of reading the whole of *A Portrait*: both are possible, though perhaps not both at the same time, and we may well need to read *A Portrait* at least twice, first in one way, then in the other.

The two modes —we can call them Mode A and Mode B— are congruent with these two entries in the diary. Mode A invites a certain degree of sympathetic identification with Stephen, a conflation of viewpoints between reader and character, and the very diary mode itself as a formal device might be regarded as offering precisely the closest identification of all, an intimacy into private thoughts; there is no other perspective, no other access.

Mode B, on the other hand, suggests a response which avoids and has no need for empathy, focussing rather upon patterns, echoes, intricacies of textual organisation rather than intimacies of character. A Mode B reader will easily have recognised and appreciated that the figs associated with Cranly indicate John the Baptist, the precursor. A Mode A reader will register that this very recognition allows Stephen to deflect his attention from, and to sidestep, the criticisms Cranly has made of him.

We can clarify the differences between these two modes of reading with some further examples and comments. A Mode A reader might well respond with sympathy and remembered identification to the adult threat made against the child Stephen on the first page or so of the novel:

> O, Stephen will apologize.
> Dante said:
> O, if not, the eagles will come and pull out his eyes.
> Pull out his eyes
> Apologize

A Mode B reader will register the beginning of a chain of allusions which will pick up in their progress not only eagles and eagle eyes, but blind bats, pandy bats, blind birds, birds of augury, herons, the bird girl wading in the water, the bird man Daedalus; eyes and blind will lead us to the broken spectacles, towards the injustice, towards Prometheus as a case of suffering injustice, Prometheus and his eagle or vulture, Prometheus meaning fore-sight (blind); the Dante reference will lead us into hell, to the pride of other identifications, with Parnell, with Lucifer (back to Prometheus), light-bearer, back to blind (lacking light), and of course to the identification with his own namesake, as Dedalus, the fall which drowns him. Moments of apologising and refusing to apologise, moments of serving and refusing to serve, of obeying and refusing to obey. Of punishment and of evasion of punishment. The Mode B reader might also want to pursue the fainter echoes of allusion, for example to Watts's now almost forgotten poem ''Obedience to Parents' with its coupling of eyes and eagles.

A Mode B reader, however, in following through such allusions, echoes and intricate inter-tracings within the texture of the novel, would no longer be responding to the novel in its diachronic organisation, its narrative movement, but as a quasi-spatial pattern, a picture, a portrait. A full Mode B reading would therefore regard the question of whether or not Stephen 'becomes' an artist as an illegitimate and even impossible question. Since 'Stephen Dedalus' is only the effect of a certain writing practice, the construct of certain motifs and themes, there isn't any future, artistic or otherwise, for any 'Stephen Dedalus' beyond the textual confines of *A Portrait.*

If, on the other hand, we read as a Mode A reader, we will have been following the novel as a peculiarly intimate representation of a young person growing up, from babyhood to the verge of adulthood. Partly by the technique of matching the style of writing to each stage of that development, we will have been brought very close to a sharing in that movement. We will have been aware of our having witnessed a growing acquisition of certain capacities in Stephen: a command over language, an education, some limited experience, albeit experience with a high degree of intensity, anguish and self-doubt. In one way or another, we will perhaps say, we have all experienced such matters.

We can all remember those moments when we scribbled our name and an address extending to the outer limits of the universe, we all have our private recall of moments of minute humiliations and minor heroisms.

We have all been through a kind of education, which perhaps mattered less than those cataclysmic childish discoveries of whatever our equivalents of sin and repentance have been. *A Portrait* invites and can sustain an extraordinary degree of identification with its central figure. And all these processes which we have seen Stephen undergoing, and which to some extent we have vicariously undergone through him, may, we recognise, be necessary to the development of 'an artist'.

There is therefore an implicit invitation to self-recognition in Stephen's notion of himself as an artist-in-process. And the flattering underlying logic of that identification is that insofar as Stephen is myself (the reader) and he is also the young Joyce, since Joyce became an artist, Stephen will become an artist: therefore I too, in this logic of the imagined, will become an artist.

However, even such an enthusiastic Mode A reader might also recognise another movement through the novel, from initial inwardness to a certain detached irony by the end, an irony which goes beyond Stephen's own, and becomes authorial. Our sympathy and identification may finally lessen faced with such final passages as this:

> *April 15.* Met her point blank in Grafton Street. The crowd brought us together. We both stopped. She asked me why I never came, said she heard all sorts of stories about me. This was only to gain time. Asked me was I writing poems? About whom? I asked her. This confused her more and I felt sorry and mean. Turned off that valve at once and opened the spiritual heroic refrigerating apparatus, invented and patented in all countries by Dante Alighieri. Talked rapidly of myself and my plans. In the midst of it unluckily made a sudden gesture of a revolutionary nature. I must have looked like a fellow throwing a handful of peas into the air. People began to look at us. She shook hands a moment after and in going away, said she hoped I would do what I said.
> Now I call that friendly, don't you?

> Yes, I liked her today. A little or much? Don't know. I liked her and it seems a new feeling to me. Then, in that case, all the rest, all that I thought I thought and all that I felt I felt, all the rest before now, in fact . . . O, give it up, old chap! Sleep it off! —
> *April 16*. Away! Away!

Despite all the acquired capacities and skills, it may be that the one thing needful which remains lacking is the love for another human being, the very question which links the conversation and the diary. Stephen's failure of language here, his retreat into ellipsis, is, like a recourse to mere swearing, an acquiescence in inadequacy, a reversion to paralysis. Given the analysis of inadequate language in *Dubliners*, this moment can enforce a decisively negative judgement.

But a Mode A reader then has a problem. If Stephen lacks what is essential to an artist, what is he to become? If all those qualities and capacities are his, except the essential, then the Mode A reader might well feel—with a certain humble superiority—that the fate actually and ironically awaiting Stephen is to become a Mode B reader, not a writer but merely a literary critic. For is not criticism the only fate for those equipped with all the appropriate literary sensibility, and the aesthetic theories and literary knowledge, but lacking the essential capacity for creation? The novel dangles that temptation before its own reader : to become only its critic—since fully to analyse *A Portrait* one almost needs the same fascination with words, the same sense of structure, the same capacity for theoretical and abstract thinking, that Stephen is equipped with.

That Stephen is eminently fitted to become a supreme exemplar of the Mode B form of reading is evidenced by several passages. For example:

> Why was he gazing upwards from the steps of the porch, hearing their shrill twofold cry, watching their flight? For an augury of good or evil? A phrase of Cornelius Agrippa flew through his mind and then there flew hither and thither shapeless thoughts from Swedenborg on the correspondence of birds to things of the intellect and of how

> the creatures of the air have their knowledge and know their times and seasons because they, unlike man, are in the order of their life and have not perverted that order by reason.
>
> And for ages men had gazed upward as he was gazing at birds in flight. The colonnade above him made him think vaguely of an ancient temple and the ashplant on which he leaned wearily of the curved stick of an augur. A sense of fear of the unknown moved in the heart of his weariness, a fear of symbols and portents, of the hawk like man whose name he bore soaring out of his captivity on osier woven wings, of Thoth, the god of writers, writing with a reed upon a tablet and bearing on his narrow ibis head the cusped moon.
>
> He smiled as he thought of the god's image for it made him think of a bottle nosed judge in a wig, putting commas into a document which he held at arm's length, and he knew that he would not have remembered the god's name but that it was like an Irish oath.

However, the reader faced with this passage, has genuinely to oscillate between two responses. Insofar as the reader re-cognises the correspondences which Stephen himself points to, and perhaps others, that reader is operating in Mode B, standing back from identificatory empathy with Stephen as character, seeing pattern rather than personality. Yet insofar as Stephen is presented as having precisely the kind of personality which sees such correspondences, the very act on the part of the reader of perceiving those same correspondences con-stitutes at another level an empathetic identification with the Stephen of the passage: a Mode A version of Mode B.

portrait of the undergraduate

Looking back upon *A Portrait*, we recognise that we could indeed have read it in two ways. But perhaps not both at once. The text requires re-reading. *A Portrait* has two kinds of reader implicit within it, those who read with the intense identification of adolescence, and those who read with the fully professional modes of academic criticism.

We can then see why *A Portrait of the Artist* is an almost too perfect text for study at university. It combines a certain attractively narcissistic mode of adolescent identification and aspiration, deeply suited to all those undergraduates who see themselves as budding Writers. It even caters to the adolescent sense that if love is what remains to be acquired, that too will—given the nature of undergraduate adolescence—not be long wanting. At the same time, *Portrait* combines this with an openness to an immensely elaborate elucidation and endless critical analysis and commentary, highly suitable to tertiary education practices of discussion and dissertation. In its precise combination of those apparently opposed practices of reading, the novel thus neatly anticipates a central development within education, and it is indeed from within that development that *A Portrait* has been so emphatic-ally endorsed. If we now probe this peculiar appropriateness of *A Portrait* somewhat further, an important twist appears.

It is of some significance in the actual process of reading *A Portrait* that we are aware that Joyce went on to become a major writer, and that *Ulysses* and *Finnegans Wake* were the books he went on to write. In particular, in reading *Ulysses* we can tend to think of Stephen as not quite yet capable of writing *Ulysses*, but of experiencing this Bloomsday with sufficient self-regarding attentiveness that, one day, he will indeed record it all in *Ulysses*. And all of us can muster up the same kind of attentiveness with regard to our own ordinary days.

At the same time, we can also see our other possible selves in Bloom, who, after all, will never write his *Ulysses*, though it is clear that the capacity to create Bloom himself is one capacity that remains beyond the scope of Stephen. We can thus identify both with the writer who hasn't yet written his masterpiece and with the non-writer who never will: both are thereby brought within our own compass, as akin to ourselves in our (only?) apparent ordinariness. Given enough hard work, and the luck of actually meeting a Nora, any reader of Stephen's age can feel capable of their own *Ulysses* and any reader of Bloom's age can feel that the possibility has existed, after all, if only once upon a long time.

Even the internal structure of the novel encourages this sense that writing novels is not much more than hard work: the second half of *Ulysses can* almost seem like a set of exercises in how to construct itself out of the first half.

More generally, we are aware, while reading *A Portrait* , what it has meant to become a great writer in the Modernist period, and on that definition, the difference between being a Joyce-like writer and being an analytical critic does not at times seem to be at all considerable, since the Joyce who wrote *Ulysses* and *Finnegans Wake* is characteristically represented as composing by a slow accumulation of working notes, by deliberate and conscious accretion of detail, by techniques of organisation, research and revision. The specifically Modernist notion of the artist is that the writer is a professional, a hard worker, a grafter. We recall Eliot's remark that if you want to be a writer after the age of twenty-five you must sweat for it; or his remark that writing a poem is like turning the leg of a table; or the phrase *'Il miglior fabbro'* (the better fabricator — or blacksmith) as the most apt tribute to Pound's revision and correction of *The Waste Land* typescript; Flaubert endlessly rewriting a sentence; Valéry investigating the precise degree to which a cliché can be revitalised by minimal linguistic engineering. All these give us our dominant image in the Modernist epoch of what the task of the writer might be seen to be. Joyce himself is notorious for having regarded creation as in some sense the original sin of the artist, and priding himself on not having 'created' anything. It's probably significant that Joyce thought that anyone could complete *Finnegans Wake* if he died prematurely (he picked James Stephens because their birthdays coincided).

But there is an ambivalence within this model of the writer. It is clearly a non-romantic notion, but it is not quite the pre-Romantic notion of the craftsman. The artist, on this model, remains in some sense special but becomes special, makes him- or her-self special, from being pretty ordinary, not by magic nor by some pre-endowed talent or genius, a gift from the gods, but by a process of deliberate work. (Kierkegaard may have been the first to popularise the idea that 90 per cent of genius is sheer hard work.)

Nor in the Joycean version of this model does the artist emerge primarily from some traditional cultural cocoon, some Establishment region of privilege of a cultural kind. Joyce did not need a country house (Coole Park) to nurture his work: a TEFL school was enough (though he too, in practice, needed an indirect source of unearned income, from patrons).

Joyce's achievement stems from a certain educational accomplishment, by attending schools and university, by going through the process of being a student. Stephen Dedalus is the first fully convincing undergraduate in fiction. He is, moreover, shown to us as not, in fact, all that much better than the average bright undergraduate. That seminar paper on *Hamlet* he delivers in *Ulysses* is probably worth a B++ grade, while his impromptu lecture on Thomist aesthetics might merit a B+++? But he is still capable (as in the diary) of making careless grammatical errors and punctuation slips. Correspondingly, the task of writing *A Portrait* or even *Ulysses* itself does not, at times, seem beyond the capacity of any not very extra-ordinary undergraduate. It is possible to take a page of *Stephen Hero* and attempt, not unsuccessfully, to re-write it as a page of *A Portrait.* It is perfectly feasible for an average class to write an extra page for, say, the Circe episode of *Ulysses.* Since we know the formidable history of the drafting of *Ulysses* and even more so of *Finnegans Wake* in all its extraordinary detail, it can at times seem (though only if we forget the novelty of the novels in their own time?) that all that is necessary is a long and sustained commitment. The very dates of composition at the end of the texts bespeak both that commitment and that invitation to emulation: *A Portrait* : 1904-1914, *Ulysses* : 1914-21.

illusions of allusion

This characteristically modernist notion of the artist can be regarded as simultaneously elitist and democratic. The apparent erudition which layers the great modernist texts, *The Waste Land* or Pound's *Cantos*, seems to exclude at first blush all but a very small minority of readers; yet at the same time the only qualification for becoming a reader of those texts is open to anyone to acquire, since it is seemingly only a matter of making oneself erudite where necessary.

The moment in *Ulysses* when Stephen Dedalus uses a crib while teaching a history lesson becomes in that respect deeply symptomatic. Those who know, even the masters of those who know, may themselves know only a certain rather limited amount. It is often an illusion that, because we have to explore whole libraries to trace an allusion, the author responsible for that allusion was actually equipped with a wide range of esoteric knowledge. The serendipidity effect of random reading can itself manufacture an effect of erudition where none is deserved.

By chance, I recently came across a summary of a 17th century novel, *The Princess Cloria* by Percy Herbert, in which the history of Ireland is allegorically related in terms of a fictional history of Crete, where the governor is called Dedalus. To claim this as a source for Joyce's odd spelling of the name would appear erudite but, whether plausible or not, resulted purely from happenstance. I once knew a scholar who regularly crawled around research libraries on his hands and knees, browsing only those books which were stacked on the floor-level shelves — on the grounds that nobody else ever bothered to reach that low, and that therefore he might stumble across forgotten but significant texts. His scholarly career presumably came to an end when he developed arthritis.

At the core of the notion that any reader has the capacity to make him- or her-self equipped adequately to read these texts, in terms at least of a knowledge of their allusions, is a curious optimism: an affirmation of the function of knowledge and education which makes it far from surprising that modernist texts have been so triumphantly associated not just with education but with an enormous expansion of education. This is not to claim that modernist writers necessarily would have approved: T. S. Eliot was notorious for recommending in the 1950s that the university intake should be reduced to well below its pre-war level. After the various post-war expansions of higher education, most students now at university do not arrive with an intimate inheritance of an intellectual cultural tradition to draw upon.

Here again, modernism lends itself most appositely to their academic and pedagogical require-ments. Modernism, unlike 18th century or even 19th century literary texts, suits such students because its puzzles are explicit, its opacities clearly signalled for the reader. In reading Shakespeare you may not be at all aware of the re-modelling of a Celtic legend or of a Plutarch anecdote; in reading Pope you may well be missing a classical allusion; while reading George Eliot you may remain ignorant of some allusion to Schopenhauer; but unless you recognise such allusions you won't know that you've missed them! In a modernist text, however, the allusions are sufficiently foregrounded (often with foreign quotations, for example, left in the original language) that you know that you have spotted that at least there *is* an allusion, though it will take you a certain amount of academic grist to enable you to see how that allusion is functioning and where it comes from. (This is not, of course, quite the same as already knowing and recognising the allusion in the first place— but that's another issue, involving a different kind of re-reading, and a different kind of pleasure.) Correspondingly, of course, this very foregrounding of the inter-textual character of modernist texts conveys a very comforting sense that such research work is how the text itself has been originally constructed anyway — which may not, of course, be the case.

It is this double sense of Stephen as both potentially an artist, a special figure, an exceptional person, and at the same time ordinary enough to be identified with, that is reinforced by his re-appearance in *Ulysses*. For at that point in his 'life' it is not the case that Stephen has actually yet become an artist, in the sense of having written a book. It would make a very considerable difference indeed to our experience of reading *Ulysses* were Stephen to be credited already with a major writing achievement. If Joyce had situated *Ulysses* at the point at which Stephen had already written his own *A Portrait of the Artist* we might have felt as readers that his capacities were beyond our emulation. But most readers of *Ulysses* can still recognise themselves in Stephen as they once were—or might have been.

In presenting us with this basic movement and ambivalence within the process of reading *A Portrait*, Joyce was deeply in tune with wider developments than simply within literature itself. In particular, that relation between the ordinary and the special becomes a structural feature of much of the mass media in the later twentieth century. Which further helps to account for the continuing resonance of *A Portrait* for a generation attuned to television.

It is the oscillation, the dialectic, the ambivalence between the 'special' and the 'ordinary', that I now want to explore in relation to TV, to what we are effectively being told about ourselves in watching television.

We are used to the notion of 'the special' programme, the 'Bing Crosby / Beatles / Take That / Madonna / Whoever / Christmas Special'— but every entertainment show on television presents itself as special, and within the show every performer deserves, we are told, a special round of applause, every personal appearance merits a special thank you, and of course every audience is, or has been, a very special audience.

Then, between the programmes, the advertisements reinforce this peculiar insistence upon the very term 'special'. Every named product in the adverts is, of course, special by comparison with all those other anonymous, every-day, ordinary washing powders, lagers, etc., and often those very products are offered in what is called a special offer or a special deal. And when the adverts are over, our attention is drawn by the TV continuity announcer to forthcoming special shows, for special occasions. These advance notices constitute a kind of advert for television by television, so it's not surprising that the use of 'special' becomes almost absurdly self referential. There is, however, one special device of ordinary product advertising which television trailers can't use of themselves: the claim that product X or event Y is special because it is 'as shown on TV'. The very fact of being seen on TV can be offered in the average advert as making the ordinary product special. Television can't explicitly appeal to this selling device for itself, though it does so implicitly all the time.

Ordinary people by appearing on quiz shows or game shows become, temporarily, special people, precisely because they are on TV. (Esther Ransom once interviewed an 80-year-old lady in a *vox pop* sequence; she—the old lady—was promptly asked to open a bazaar the following week..) For the duration of their 'spot' we watch them —and if we're watching them, they must be special. Of course, other people become somehow permanently (well, for a time) special because they are often (for a time) on TV—and, it would appear, for no other reason than that: the media personality, the TV celebrity, is a very special kind of pretty ordinary product.

Conversely, what TV can also show us is that the stars, those Very Special People, are really quite ordinary, like you or me. A somewhat similar procedure, but in a very special way, is applied to Royalty.

This entire structure implies, however, that you and I are not ordinary at all, partly because we too could have been on television in a variety of audience participation or local visit programmes, beginning with *Jim'll Fix It* when we were three years old or so, and then graduating to, say, *Down Your Way*, *Songs of Praise*, *Big Brother*, a talent *(sic)* show, or perhaps simply the local news interview with the milkman who went to Patagonia (I saw that one yesterday). And partly because, after all, while we're watching, we must be special, a very special audience — otherwise who is all this special entertainment provided for anyway?

While we watch the television we are indeed endowed with or interpellated by those presenters, chat-show hosts, and assorted celebrities, as possessing a certain special quality: we are often addressed as experts; we are a special audience because our knowledge is apparently omniscient: we are, naturally, expected to know the answers when the quiz-show contestants don't, and it is for our instantly expert appraisal that the slow motion replay is offered while the confirmatory, rather than simply informative, voice of the commentator quietly reassures us in our knowledge, a knowledge and expertise that the very process of watching, particularly in slow motion, does indeed make to some extent actual (theoretically) even while making it possible.

For that reason, if for no other, sporting commentary in particular involves difficult questions of tonal tact and servility. I know one cricket commentator, no older than myself, who now seems convinced by his own reverential adherence to the codes of BBC cricket (the 'fill-in' gossip, when the rain drizzles down), that he personally once witnessed every pre-war Test match.

The paradox, the instability, the contradiction, the almost immediate self-deconstruction, of claims to special status on television lies in the palpable fact that all these special shows, special stars and special programmes constitute that everyday, very ordinary, wholly unexceptional activity of 'watching the telly'.

To illustrate this process, I've taken one special day, August Bank Holiday: 26th August 1985. Quotations are from the programme descriptions in the *TV Times* and *Radio Times* for that day.

The determined viewer might have settled down to something like the following programming, by conscientiously switching channels:

2.40 BBC2: *Destry Rides Again*, a film starring Marlene Dietrich and James Stewart, the latter playing Destry, a seemingly shy sheriff, a pretty ordinary man, who of course proves not to be at all ordinary.

Followed at 4.10 by *Windmill Bank Holiday Special* and at 5.10 by the film *The Barefoot Contessa* starring Humphrey Bogart and Eva Gardner, in which 'Harry Dawes, a Hollywood director, discovers flamenco dancer Maria Vargas in a tawdry Madrid nightclub and turns her into a star', etc.

Quickly tiring of that, switch at 5.30 to Channel 4: *Everyone A Special Kind Of Artist* in which 'ex Durham miner, now a poet, Jock Purdon writes and sings all his own material. Also featured is Tom McGuiness, another ex miner, whose paintings and etchings illustrate Jock's songs.'

Alternatively, at 5.35 we could catch *The Making of Superman III* (a very special guy), in anticipation of of the 7 o'clock programme *The Krypton Factor*, 'bringing together two ordinary men and two ordinary women to confront the savagely demanding tests of television's toughest quiz.' Of course, by simply appearing. these ordinary men and women might prove themselves rather special

If, however, we stayed with *Everyone a Special Kind of Artist* we could watch, at 6.15, *Jim'll Fix It*, in which we could 'see Christopher as a five year old Dr Kildare; hear Louise slam 100 doors; watch David as a ten year old butler; marvel as Nicola turns into Wonder Woman.' Since this was a special birthday celebration for the show we can even see some special re-transmissions from the past ten years.

After a short break for tea we can watch *Jim Davidson's Special* at 8 pm, followed by the film *Death Trap*, starring Christopher Reeve (no longer Superman), Michael Caine and Dyan Cannon 'in which a celebrated playwright seems to be confronted by a former drama student who has now written a first-class mystery play and is about to replace Sidney'as a very special playwright.

Tiring of that, one could switch over at 10.5 for *Bob Monkhouse Meets Joan Rivers*: 'another chance to see the special programme in which Bob Monkhouse welcomes back to these shores Joan Rivers. Also featuring their special musical guests Frankie Goes to Hollywood'.

But that would mean missing the *News at Ten*, and since every day, even August Bank Holiday, something special has to have happened, to justify *The News*, it would probably be a pity to have missed it.

What kind of link is there between the two modes of reading Joyce's *Portrait* and the ambivalence of the word 'special' in relation to television? We can only too easily imagine the Hollywood or made-for-TV film version of *A Portrait,* which would slot very neatly into the Bank Holiday schedule. For there is a certain consonance at the point of reception, rather than of production. In reading Joyce it is important to the dialectic of ordinary/special that I am reading what would be the end- product of being special in the way that Stephen wants to be. If I too were special in that special way, I too would be capable of writing what I am reading.

Just as in watching television, part at least of the dialectic of ordinary/special rests upon the explicit claim that being on television is somehow a special thing to be, and yet that television is—as we know, since we are watching it—basically a perfectly ordinary activity in our lives. Therefore, we could, much of the time, be the ones doing what we are watching. A chat show in a theatre or a novel about a footballer would not have quite the same effect, an effect I want to label 'reflexive'. Reflexive reading or reflexive watching incorporates us within the oscillations set up between the ordinariness and the specialness of what we are reading or watching.

In one sense, to be on television is indeed special: it is out of the ordinary, not just in the sense that we don't do it all the time, but that appearing on television is now a professional domain, a special-ist job, requiring and providing trained special-isms. Yet there seems to be an endemic strain between fully acknowledging the professional status and competence required for appearing regularly on television, and demanding a much wider 'access' on television. Some Channel 4 presenters, in particular, seem to find difficult the relationship between their own professional status and the air of allowing ordinary viewers some increased say in the ethos of the channel. The very hesitation between formal and informal modes of address by announcers indicates a certain trembling across that difficulty.

There is even a partial parallel here with literacy itself, with the interplay between reading and writing. Some experiences of reading (perhaps this one) produce exactly that sense that 'I could have written this' —which is one of the levels at which *Portrait* appeals to its readers. In other words, the differentiation between those who appear on television, those who 'write', who are special, and those who don't appear or write, who aren't special, needs to be resolved. It is ideologically resolved, in many cases, by appeal to the category of 'talent' or 'genius'. What differentiates those who do and those who don't, those who appear and those who don't appear, is to be explained by the elusive quality of talent. Yet it seems clear not only that Joyce's work, precisely as work, undermines that ideological move, but that television more or less refutes it by its very practice: considerable numbers of decidedly untalented people (if we allow the term at all) seem to be given the run of the studios.

Joyce's whole *oeuvre* insists upon labour, not talent, upon the *work* of composition, upon the calculable thousands of hours spent composing *Ulysses*. This is one aspect of the work-ethic: the implication of a fixed ratio between time, effort and money. But Stephen, uneasy with both the strategy of saving and the advice never to owe, knows, as any student or teacher knows, that there is in fact no exact ratio between effort and reward—or rather that there cannot be a ratio between the hours spent tackling an intellectual or creative problem and the probability of it being resolved. This seems, often, a matter of chance or luck rather than of determination or decision.

At some fundamental level, we are aware that no matter how many hours we put into the composition of an essay, or a book, it is not the number of hours which will guarantee the quality of the result. But nor is it a matter simply of 'talent', since any such alleged quality certainly doesn't act as a reliable guarantee either.

Part of the point of *Ulysses* would appear to be that a single day, for example, is not a unit of value. One could make a 700-page novel out of any one day just as readily as one could make a seven-page short story—though the mere fact of the novel being 700 pages long doesn't make it a good novel.

Conversely, television by making the production of art, entertainment, and ideas—all those areas for 'talented performance'—into a daily, repeated, exactly timed, and precisely scheduled professional job, thereby deeply undermines our sense that talent does indeed escape the work-ethic, the structure of commissioned and regulated labour, of simply hack work.

an ordinary day

In the core gesture of *Ulysses* there is an even more extraordinary affirmation of the relation between the ordinary and the special. This 700-page treatment of one day is, after all, concerned with June 16th 1904, that day now known as Bloomsday. It was not the date of a battle or of a treaty, a coronation or a conquest, a regal death or a general slaughter, but of an encounter between a man and a woman. In becoming a turning point in the history of the novel, June 16th indicates that any day can be a special day, can be made into a turning point. Just as on Easter Monday 1916 in Dublin, a perfectly ordinary day was turned, it seemed, into a special event.

James Stephens has a haunting account of that now memorable day, as it began in banality:

> On the morning following I awoke into full insurrection and bloody war, but I did not know anything about it. It was Bank Holiday, but for employments such as mine there are not any holidays, so I went to my office at the usual hour . .
>
> At one o'clock I went to lunch. Passing the corner of Merrion Row I saw two small groups of people. These people were regarding steadfastly in the direction of St. Stephen's Green Park, and they spoke occasionally to one another with that detached confidence which proved they were mutually unknown. I also, but without approaching them, stared in the direction of the Green. I saw nothing but the narrow street which widened to the Park. ..

> On the way home I noticed that many silent people were standing in their doorways — an unusual thing in Dublin outside of the back streets . . I felt faintly uneasy but withdrew my mind to a meditation which I had covenanted with myself to perform daily, and passed to my house.
>
> There I was told that there had been a great deal of rifle firing all the morning, and we concluded that the Military recruits or Volunteer detachments were practising that a.m. My return to business was by the way I had come. At the corner of Merrion Square I found the same silent groups, who were still addressing each other occasionally with the detached confidence of strangers.
>
> "Has there been an accident?" said I...
>
> "Don't you know? " . .
>
> And then he saw that I did not know.
>
> "The Sinn Feiners have seized the City this morning."
>
> "Oh!" said I.

An ordinary Bank Holiday can become a historic date. Conversely, a date that might have become historic can remain merely a missed opportunity. I am reminded of a postscript to an article, written just over a year after the Easter rising:

> The above lines were written on Friday, September 1, but due to unforseen circumstances they did not reach the editorial office that day. After reading Saturday's and today's (Sunday's) papers, I say to myself: perhaps it is already too late to offer a compromise. Perhaps the few days in which a peaceful development was still possible have passed too. Yes, to all intents and purposes they have passed . . All that remains is to send these notes to the editor with the request to have them entitled 'Belated Thoughts'. Perhaps even belated thoughts are sometimes not without interest.

The article was entitled 'On Compromises', and suggested one. The delayed date of publication was September 3rd 1917, and the journalist was V. I. Lenin.

The reason why June 16th 1904 is special in *Ulysses* presumably has to do with Joyce meeting Nora on that date. If the inability to find a love is crucial to *Portrait* and the finding of it lies behind *Ulysses*, this is partly because love and loving are also variations on the dialectic of ordinary and special. Love is a specialisation of the ordinary. The loved one is special, even if to everyone else the beloved is wholly ordinary. Some familiar problems that fascinate novelists and dramatists arise when the same person becomes special to more than one lover. By choice and chance, Joyce found his love. Stephen perhaps missed his opportunity: he leaves for exile, silence, and cunning, but also loneliness, on April 27th. Nora did not appear till June.

Family relations are also ordinarily special. For every parent, their own child is different from all others; for every child their own parent is different from others. The full recognition of the absolute ordinariness, the fully common condition, of a parent or of a child, may only arrive with their death, if at all. It is possible also, from exile, to recognise that one's own city is a pretty ordinary city, while it nevertheless remains a special city for you.

What is involved in both cases is the relation between a given-ness and a point-of-view : the very given location from which we learned to see the world at all. Television, in generalising our shared view-point, in giving us an easily roving eye, a perspective which is no longer special, no longer a matter of being fixed and rooted but of a mobile and global eye, has perhaps undermined and replaced that older dialetic between special and ordinary view-point. We can all seem exiles from everywhere.

Global television perhaps helped, for a time, to replace local loyalties and identifications with a quite new perspective: that whereby the globe itself, seen in its slow spinning, from the supreme aerial view-point of high space, can be seen as merely another planet in the black emptiness.

A cosmic awareness may insist that our star is only one among ten thousand billion, but three kilometres of atmosphere make this planet undeniably special for us. Each of us, like Stephen, has written a childhood address which begins with our family name and ends with the universe itself. And, increasingly, each of us can ask, with Yeats' poem, 'Upon a House Shaken by the Land Agitation', 'How should the world be luckier...? '

Each of us can see our self as special; that is our perhaps necessary view-point. And perhaps every country imagines itself at the centre of its global atlas. But the logic of claiming that everybody is equally special has rested upon either a religious affirmation (God's viewpoint: every soul is created equal in the eyes of a God) or a radical egalitarianism. The slow drift from the mass slaughters of World War I to the potential global genocide of World War III, in which everyone will be equal in the nuclear winter, has perhaps dented that affirmation: the ordinary city of Hiroshima on that banal August morning of 1945 has left us with a new sense of our equal citizenship in the city of the dead. Or our equal citizenship in a single and endangered globe.

The affirmation of everyone's potential equality found a new mode of expression in that characteristic genre of the epoch of radical egalitarianism: the autobiography, a term from the decade of the French Revolution. Henceforth, it can seem, everybody has at least one book to write, the book of their own life: a portrait of the author as young. But another logic emerges here. Once that book is written, it too becomes simply another ordinary publication. To produce the truly special book, in this post-Romantic logic, is to produce the radically new, the summation and transcendence of all that precedes, from Homer to Meredith, from Sophocles to Ibsen.

But even then the logic of 'special' demands another step: the cosmic text, the summation of everything, the book in which Here Comes Everybody, in which not even one's own language retains its special character but all languages are equal and language itself is made anew.

Joyce's trajectory seems to me caught in this logic, from the moment that he presented his own starting point in *Dubliners*. It can seem a radically individualist, even Protestant, stance and creed: a relation between the equal but single individual and the cosmos itself, without mediation of nation or class: a curiously abstract soul under inter-national socialism. But the normal logic of love is not individual but social, a matter of marriage in one of its many forms. Though Joyce and Nora refused the specific marital institutional form available in Catholic Ireland, Joyce's next book was to celebrate a married couple, ordinary in their every-day-ness. As such, it could be another contribution to changing a moral history in which, for example, Parnell had once been destroyed because of an every-day variation on marriage.

A year after *Portrait* appeared, W.B. Yeats also finally got married, but not to his long-intended Maud Gonne. In what must have seemed an extraordinary example of moral luck, his marriage promptly provided him with his own cosmic work, and not through the dedicated labours of a Joyce: Georgie Hyde Lees' automatic writing seemed, to Yeats, to have brought what the whole world was awaiting, a new perspective upon the whole of history, an ultimate Vision. A matter of Choice and Chance.

On the final page or so of *A Portrait*, in his diary entry for April 6th, Stephen acknowledges that other rival presence:

> Michael Robartes remembers forgotten beauty and, when his arms wrap her round, he presses in his arms the loveliness which has long faded from the world. Not this. Not at all. I desire to press in my arms the loveliness which has not yet come into the world.

In 1921 Yeats published a new volume of poems, entitled *Michael Robartes and the Dancer*, which was to be carefully shaped around both marriage—the choice and chance of love—and history—the choice and chance of politics—but also the cosmic and epochal. The volume finally included full publication of the poem of that now extra-ordinary day, 'Easter 1916'.

A year later Joyce immortalised his own special day: June 16th 1904. Nora's day. Bloomsday.

*

ULYSSES, 1914 - 1921: ALGEBRA AND CEATION

Nestor

In the second episode of *Ulysses* Stephen Dedalus gives a history lesson:

> You, Cochrane, what city sent for him?

Neither Cochrane nor Stephen know all the answers. Stephen, like his pupils, has to consult a crib:

> Asculum, Stephen said, glancing at the name and date in the gorescarred book.

Yet the details of time and place, date and town, matter less perhaps than the phrase the world has remembered from that battle, remembered because it could have been said by any general to any officers; any time, any place, any occasion that fitted the phrase could have originated the phrase: Another victory like that and we are done for. For history recurs, similarities return. A boy who lives on Vico Road—named with the name of the philosopher of historical recurrence—eats fig-rolls as an earlier student, in an earlier book, also did. The artist can repeat motifs, remember a re-applicable touch of the symbolic. Precursors too recur.

But history may also have a direction, even if it has no end, a disappointed bridge. Dun Laoghaire pier recalls a specific history, unrepeatable moment: Kings-town. A common name, any king, any town. But also this place, that time. Permanent in its present effects, continuing, undeniable. A fact of the past:

> Had Pyrrhus not fallen by a beldam's hand
> or Julius Caesar not been knifed to death?

Such events happened in some way even if not as memory has fabled them. They are not to be thought away. History may be a tale like any other, but certain possibilities become actual. Time has branded them and, fettered, they are lodged in the room of the infinite possibilities they have ousted.

But how does the possible render other possibilities no longer possible, an infinity of future eventualities swept aside by the one occurrence that was actual? Asculum. 279 BC. And that phrase, spoken, then.

Can those other possibilities have actually been possible seeing that they never were? Or was that only possible which came to pass? A not unimportant question for an Irishman in 1917. Are options an illusion only, what happens wholly predetermined, multiple possibilities pre-cluded, the rose-garden, the path we did not take? If a pupil asks for a ghoststory and Stephen refuses, opening another book, for the predetermined lesson—no longer history, with its palpable problems, but the safer ground (surely) of literature—is it inevitable that Milton's poem he alights upon should be, after all, a kind of ghost-story?

> Lycidas, your sorrow, is not dead
> Sunk though he be beneath the watery floor?

Lines from Milton's elegy for the dead minor poet, Edward King (again), drowned while crossing the Irish sea in 1637. But was it possible that Milton himself might have died, in 1637. Some mute inglorious Miltons are mute because they died before their time. As Pound registered in 1917: some died *pro patria*, for an old bitch gone in the teeth, for a case full of battered books. A not unimportant consideration for a not yet great Irish writer trying to live out the Great War in neutral Switzerland.

In a novel, perhaps, all is planned, both recurring motifs and plot directions, echoes of other sorrows, other drowned men, all tiny steps in a forward movement of reading, a movement of writing. But it is not pre-determined, surely, that the novel itself gets written? This novel? Might *Paradise Lost* have never been written, John Milton (d. 1637) remembered only in an early elegy by that major English epic poet Edward King (d. 1674)? But would then the history of the Cromwellian period also have been different, with no Defender of the English People, no combative justifier of regicide? And with that change in Cromwell's fortunes, perhaps a change in those of Ireland too?

And the history, sir?
After, Stephen said.

What does history come after? Where do you begin in this?

And another phrase the world has remembered: It must be a movement, then, an actuality of the possible as possible. Aristotle's phrase, remembered, from a Paris library where a delicate Siamese conned a handbook of strategy, planning perhaps his own future Pyrrhic victory, perhaps a Thai 1916, the effects of which—if perhaps the reforming monarch Chulalongkorn (reigned 1868-1910) had been ousted—would have changed South-East Asian history. (In 1911 a young Vietnamese studied strategy in Paris.) Aristotle thought poetry more philosophical than history. And a young Stephen remembers a younger Stephen's thought, emerging from the mind's darkness: Thought is the thought of thought. Tranquil brightness. Insight. The soul, therefore, is in a manner all that is: the soul is the form of forms. Tranquillity sudden, vast, candescent: form of forms. Insight of insight. But how does thought occur where thought was not, displacing darkness, other myriad possibilities, other possible thoughts? Thought from thought, a closed circle of inner illumination—is that the process? Or pursuit, directed reading, studious silence, feeding brains? Or serendipity, reading two pages apiece of seven books every night, promiscuous curiosity, accidental *aperçus*? Thought of thought.

A chain of thought, broken, interrupted:

Talbot repeated:
— Through the dear might of Him that walked the waves.

Providential impossibility. Physical miracle. And the poem? Gift or graft? Render unto God and unto Caesar. Spirit or sweat. A riddle.

Riddle me, riddle me, randy ro.
My father gave me seeds to sow.

But do thoughts come, naturally, from feeding brains, with faintly beating feelers, or, mysteriously, from the soul, form of forms?

A difficult conception, either way. What fathers thought?

> Do you understand how to do them now? he asked.

Copying sums from a board is not to understand them, to know how to do them oneself. The peculiar task of the teacher, to make understanding actual where before it was only possible, if possible. Sitting at his side Stephen solved out the problem. But his own problem does not yield to numbers. He proves by algebra that Shakespeare's ghost is Hamlet's grandfather, but the question of a father's seed and a mother's love yield neither to arithmetic nor to grammar, neither physiology nor logic:

> Ugly and futile: lean neck and tangled hair... Yet someone had loved him. Was that then real? The only true thing in life?

Amor matris, love of mother: subjective and objective genitive. Is reciprocity only possible? Like him was I. My childhood bends beside me. Yet now a ghost-mother comes to haunt, only in dreams, a lost love un-returned. A poor soul gone to heaven. Or just a twig burnt in the fire, the only real thing gone in ashes. The secret behind the eyes. The sum was done. *Ego sum*, the sum of body and soul, yet another I: a secret hidden even from our own eyes, even from our own I. Is that I already its future, albeit not known? How is the possible possible? A teacher in a school, a future Deasy, or an artist in the making? A young man's questions, any time, any place. That school, but known to all men.

> Very good. Well?
> There was a battle, sir.
> Very good. Where?

. . . .

> Cochrane and Halliday are on the same side, sir, Stephen cried.

The teacher's tones carry the complaint of the schoolboy, still. And his ears still will hear the echoes as a schoolboy would:

Will you wait in my study for a moment, Mr. Deasy said.

As it was in the beginning, is now, and ever shall be, for a schoolboy's world without end. The study. The schoolboy. Recurrence. The open future already closed. Unless. The same room and hour, the same wisdom: and I the same. Three times now. Three nooses round me here. I can break them in this instance if I will. If that possibility is possible. But that is not a matter just to be thought away; willed away, otherwise I will remain fettered, lodged in this room of only possibilities. Nor does the same, old, wisdom appeal: Save. Salvation. Money is power, already that of someone else. So saving is a Pyrrhic strategy. Vain pretence to keep and hoard. Time surely would indeed scatter all. No great goal.

Our Mr. Deasy is a writer too, already, seeking to change events, preventatively, in anticipation. Scientifically. A contribution to Ireland. Almost all his history is wrong. So too was his science, even then. And his writing is, we think, predictable. But he knows the future. I forsee, said Mr. Deasy, that you will not remain here very long at this work. The novel confirms his knowledge. But is anybody born to be a teacher or born to be an artist? My father gave me seeds to sow. But does the I, after all that, owe only a kind of nothing?

Telemachus

— You're not a believer, are you? Haines asked. I mean, a believer in the narrow sense of the word. Creation from nothing and miracles and a personal God.
— There's only one sense of the word, it seems to me, Stephen said.

But is the creation from nothing that made the world the same as the creation from nothing which makes each and every soul and is that creation simply the same as that act whereby God the Father begets the Son? The heresies multiply, Photius and Arius, warring life-long upon the con-substantiality of the Son with the Father, and Valentine, spurning Christ's terrene body, and the subtle African heresiarch Sabellius who held that the Father was Himself His own Son.

Algebra of theology. Algebra of creation. He proves by algebra that Hamlet's grandson is Shakespeare's grandfather and that he himself is the ghost of his own father. Creation from nothing. The void awaits surely all of them that weave the wind.

Or was that only possible which came to pass? Weave, weaver of the wind.
— Tell us a story, sir.

Where do little stories come from? If Stephen is to tell us stories, will they be made up or be-gotten, created or manufactured? And what, after all, is the difference? Like thoughts of thoughts, made from other thoughts, yet new, not having existed before, though—necessarily?—possible before actual, a move across the void which awaits all those who try to un-riddle the mystery. And if history is to blame, how is history possible, a history out of history, yet new, now, awaiting possibility. A new Easter, 1916. (As Telemachus was completed, in the November of 1917, another history began with a Lenin once perhaps met in Zurich. Chancer. Chance. Perhaps.)

—After all, I should think you are able to free yourself. You are your own master, it seems to me.
—I am the servant of two masters, Stephen said.

I will not serve, an earlier Stephen had said, an earlier book. So I carried the boat of incense at Clongowes. I am another now and yet the same. A servant too. A servant of a servant. Here I am. A place, a time, a date. Between before and after, always. But can the I free the I? A matter of will? Will's way. A matter of chance? Chance or choice. A matter of birth? Or does nothing of that matter? A void, a mystery. *Ex nihilo*. Creation from nothing. Nothing from nothing.

Yet the story is told, is under way, has begun. Stately, plump Buck Mulligan came from the stairhead. *Introibo*. A ritual beginning. Before that phrase, a blank, a silence, a void. Or: another novel, a portrait of another Stephen, this one the same yet different, another imagined world.

Or: other texts, other drafts, corrections, revisions, erasures, a making and manufacturing. Stephen's history comes after a lot of work. But where do you begin in this? How does the born servant, not born to be a teacher, become a master? Creation from nothing? Self-begotten? Made in Dublin?

Proteus

Am I walking into eternity along Sandymount Strand? A direction, uni-linear, given, fated unto death. But first? And before and after? There all the time without you: and ever shall be, world without end. But in-between? I, now.

History is a nightmare from which I am trying to awake.

But how do you wake up, wake yourself up? Will? Chance? An alarm ringing you out of sleep? You cannot watch yourself wake up. You just do. Now. Open your eyes now. I will. One moment. See now. Simple action, if it is only a matter of opening the eyes. Ineluctable modality of the visible. Aristotle's phrases. But he adds: in bodies. Then he was aware of them bodies before of them coloured. How? By knocking his head against them, sure. Simple matter. If it's only a matter of bodies, bodies of matter. Dogsbodies. That great gaol.

But is it only a matter of bodies? One of her sisterhood lugged me into life. But: creation from nothing? The cords of all creations link back, strandentwining cable of all flesh. I was, too, made not begotten. By them, they clasped and sundered. But: from before the ages He willed me and now may not will me away for ever. Act of will. *Ex nihilo.*

That me. Or other me? The possibilities. Am I going to Aunt Sara's or not? A bolt drawn back and Walter welcomes me. We thought you were someone else. Exactly so. All this happens in imagination, in writing, a possibility not fully realised. Alongside others, in that room of more or less infinite possibilities, in a text. You told the Clongowes gentry you had an uncle a judge and an uncle a general in the army. Cousin Stephen, you will never be a saint. Not in my book.

You were going to do wonders, what? Missionary to Europe after fiery Columbanus. All in imagination, like the *alibi* if they arrested you for murder somewhere; like the hired dog you shot to pieces in the post office; like the Kevin Egan you might have become if your past had been different and another Post Office had been otherwise (by 1921). (But how was that Post Office possible, in 1916, in the first place?) *Lui, c'est moi.* All in imagination, in a text.

And remember your epiphanies, copies to be sent if you died to all the libraries of the world, including Alexandria? But if Stephen D. had died young, like a possible Milton, his epiphanies might have been in an imagined Alexandria (in, say, the story by Buck Mulligan known as *Odysseus*) but we would not now be reading *Ulysses*—in which Stephen D. did not die young. Though S. D. did not in any case die, either young or old. Only in imagination, in a book. Another story.

Meanwhile, I have passed the way to Aunt Sara's. Am I going there? Seems not. A matter of chance, fated—that I should continue on my way, a different day from that other possible June 16th, a day at Aunt Sara's. Another story too.

From all this came scribbled words, considered words, rejected words, not fully rejected since we read them; but we have to wait another eighty or so pages for Stephen's sixteen chosen words, his first poem (in this book): Who ever anywhere will read these written words? Not yet, not for another eighty pages. But still, these written words, asking who will read them as we actually do so (is that possible?). And when one reads these strange pages of one long gone one feels that one is at one with one who once . . .

Lui, c'est moi, walking into eternity along a Sandymount Strand, once. That I might have done, have done indeed. An Irish holiday. But those words I have not written. Copied, yes. Trans-scribed. Those words. Stephen writes a poem, as who has not? But writing the poem is not—is it?—like opening your eyes, like running your head against a body, even like waking up; nor is it like going, or not going, to Aunt Sara's—on which a whole history can hinge (a Nora Barnacle perhaps: God becomes man becomes fish becomes barnacle goose . . .).

But it is like writing: Am I walking into eternity along Sandymount Strand? Physically, that is. And other possibilities of producing texts. Like writing *Hamlet*. Again.

Scylla and Charybdis

It is this hour of the day in mid-June, in mid-*Ulysses*, and AE objects to the opening moves of Stephen D.'s *Hamlet* algebra. Peeping and prying into greenroom gossip of the day, the poet's drinking, the poet's debt. We have *King Lear*: and it is immortal. Art has to reveal to us ideas, formless spiritual essences. But: See this. Remember. Listen:

> Young Colum and Starkey. George Roberts is doing the commercial part. Longworth will give it a good puff in the Express. O, will he? I liked Colum's *Drover*. Yes, I think he has that queer thing, genius. Do you think he has genius, really? Yeats admired his line: *As in wild earth a Grecian vase*. Did he? I hope you'll be able to come tonight. Malachi Mulligan is coming too. Moore asked him to bring Haines. Did you hear Miss Mitchell's joke about Moore and Martyn? That Moore is Martyn's wild oats? Awfully clever, isn't it? They remind one of don Quixote and Sancho Panza. Our national epic has yet to be written . .

No longer and not yet. Seen, remembered, written, library literary gossip re-created in Ireland's *Ulysses*. In the intense instant of imagination, that which I was is that which I am and that which in possibility I may come to be. So in the future, sister of the past, I may see myself as I sit here now but by reflection from that which then I shall be. Thus, discussing William Shakespeare and company, Limited, the people's Will, in a book published by Shakespeare & Co. That is Will's way. We should not now combine a Norse saga with an excerpt from a novel by George Meredith. He puts Bohemia on the seacoast and makes Ulysses quote Aristotle.

So we read in a *Ulysses* which quotes Aristotle and combines a Greek epic with a telegram lifted from a George Meredith novel. Even Eglinton, objecting to Stephen's way with names in Shakespeare, appeals to Stephen's own name to explain his fantastical humour. Thus, Will's way. Thus, this novel turns upon itself reflexively, an outcome from a past which it re-imagines in order to leave open the future from which it is imagined as one day becoming. Stephen is by no means Joyce, did not write *Ulysses*, but might one day have done so, in imagination, his own or Joyce's.

Nevertheless, he has the poet's debts, Joyce's own. Literally and metaphorically. Drummond of Hawthornden helped him at that style.

> Do you intend to pay it back?
> O, yes.
> When? Now?
> Well . . . no.
> When, then?
> I paid my way. I paid my way.

The last sixteen perfectly balanced, chosen words.

> Wait. Five months. Molecules all change. I am other I now.
> Other I got pound.
> Buzz. Buzz.
> But I, entelechy, form of forms, am I by memory because under everchanging forms.
> I that sinned and prayed and fasted.
> A child Conmee saved from pandies.
> I, I and I. I.
> A.E.I.O.U.

A pound owed (IOU) to Russell (AE). And the five vowels. And the four scholastic, Aristotelian, logical possibilities: Universal Affirmative (A: all A are B); Universal Negative (E: no A are B); Particular Affirmative (I: some A are B); Particular Negative (O: no A are B). But U? Algebra of logic: I am You?

Or logically impossible arithmetical I, made by adding I and I and I. Am I from another novel? Everchanging. Are U? And here he ponders things that were not: what Caesar would have lived to do had he believed the soothsayer: what might have been: possibilities of the possible as possible.

Maeterlinck says: *If Socrates leave his house today he will find the sage seated on his doorstep.* Someone adds: Every life is many days, day after day. A day in mid-June. The 16th. We walk through ourselves, meeting robbers, ghosts, giants, old men, young men, wives, widows, brothers-in-love. But always meeting ourselves.

He found in the world without as actual what was in his world within as possible. And possibilities of the possible as possible. What Stephen might have lived to do. Molecules all change. I am other I now. Strange logic of actual, possible. I owe you. Necessity, says an Aristotelian dagger-definition, is that in virtue of which it is impossible that one can be otherwise. Strange necessity.

As Socrates leaves his portals he might discover a sage seated on the step. What useful discovery did Socrates learn from Xanthippe? Wife-shrew. Dialectic, skill in argument, answered Stephen. And from his mother (mid-wife) how to bring thoughts into the world. Where do little thoughts come from? *Inventio*, dialectic, logic, rhetoric. Mother and father of invention. But fatherhood in the sense of conscious begetting is unknown to men. It is a mystical estate, an apostolic succession, from only begetter to only begotten. On that mystery, upon incertitude, upon unlikelihood, like the world, macro- and micro-cosm, upon the void, a legal fiction, *Ulysses*—this little world of fiction, this strange imagining of possibilities—rests, weaver of the wind.

> What the hell are you driving at?
> I know. Shut up. Blast you! I have reasons.
> *Amplius. Adhuc. Iterum. Postea.*

Aquinas's rubrics for steps in an argument, logical, dialectical, rational. But is Stephen's logic not what we might call logical?

The intense instant of imagination crosses with the instant of blind rut. Am I father? If I were? The endless possibilities: Georgina Johnson, clergyman's daughter, mother-to-be of poet's off-sprung bye-blow.

The voices oscillate, Joycean, Dedalan. If Stephen were going to be the author of an *Ulysses* would Joyce, as a young man, be his own grandson? When Rutlandbaconsouthampton-shakespeare or another poet of the same name wrote *Hamlet* he was not the father of his own son merely, but being no more a son, he was and felt himself to be the father of all his race, the father of his own grandfather, the father of his unborn grandson who, by the same token, never was born . . . Missed opportunity.

> — You are a delusion, said roundly John Eglinton to Stephen. Do you believe your own story?
> — No, Stephen said promptly.
> — Are you going to write it? Mr. Best asked. You ought to make it a dialogue, don't you know.

Yes, we know, we've read the book. But how does : One day in the national library we had a discussion. Shakes. become : 'the most beautiful book that has come out of our country in my time. One thinks of Homer'? Not Lady Gregory, that old hake Augusta Gregory, but Jimmy Augusta Joyce, mis-christened, made in Dublin, re-made June 16th 1904. Dublin 1914 — Trieste 1921. Place, Date. History. Where do little big books come from?

As we read, it is constantly impossible to forget that Joyce, author of *Ulysses*, is not Stephen Dedalus, character in *Ulysses*, yet impossible not to know that the novel here turns its reflexive criticism upon the void of its own invention, constantly alerts us that *Ulysses* came from *this*; if not as this story has fabled it, it was in some way thus; yet the theory that such facts explain this fiction is refused, within the fiction that proposes it. Have we been brought all this way for a nothing? Or do we know the answer already, having read that other book from which it came, in a manner of speaking?

One strange Thomistic necessity remains, to recur: *Amplius. In societate humana hoc est maxime necessarium ut sit amicitia inter multos.* In human society this is the most necessary, that there should be *amicitia* between many. Friendship. Love. A new logic of I and I and I. An algebra of I am We. Another great goal. A possibility. Perhaps. Some time. Some place.

*

Comment?

These preceding fragments of accompaniment as commentary will already have demonstrated that familiar temptation which haunts any attempt to write criticism of Joyce's work: the temptation simply to reproduce the text of that work, as quotation; to hope that elucidation and illumination will be effected simply by arranging juxtapositions of material from Joyce's own text. The reason for this temptation is fairly obvious: anyone who has ever taught Joyce's work, particularly in a lively seminar, will have realised that the material is of such density, in allusions and echoes across the entire *oeuvre*, that any single short passage will yield enough material for two hour's discussion. Knowing this, it can well be thought that any attempt to reproduce in one's own writing those complex layers of resonance—which multi-voiced and meandering discussion can more easily handle—is bound to fail.

In dealing with those sections dominated by Stephen, moreover, that temptation is reinforced by the intensity of identification which can occur between the reader and Stephen. It is not simply that Joyce's way of presenting Stephen—the 'stream of consciousness' techniques about which we once had to learn—encourages an immediate assimilation of Stephen's 'voice' to our own as we read. It is also the case, I think, that Stephen's concerns are characteristic of the adolescent preoccupations likely to have been shared by those very readers.

Any reader involved in an engaged reading of *Ulysses* is likely either to be an adolescent having to study the novel within an educational apparatus, to be a student, and therefore to a large extent of an age with Stephen himself (though differences of gender are perhaps of more importance here than I can easily imagine); or to have once been the kind of adolescent Stephen still is, one who imagines himself (or herself) as *possibly* one day becoming a writer.The very fact that I am attempting to write about Joyce, and that you are reading this attempt, perhaps reinforces my contention that we are both likely to identify, at least *via* the memory of our own youth, with those concerns and preoccupations of Stephen the budding (he hopes) writer.
Thus, in the preceding sections, my own way of writing has been assimilated to and has incorporated Stephen's way of talking to himself, enacting that degree of remembered identification I acknowledge to occur as I read these sections.

Yet there is, of course, a difficulty in writing criticism in this way. For the reader of that criticism has already to know the text of *Ulysses* very well indeed in order to recognise the quasi-quotation, to see the point of the juxtapositions offered, even to recognise that an assimilation of styles is occurring. To hear the conflation of my voice and that of Dedalus in the first place, and then to discriminate between those two voices, would seem to require a reader who probably has no need of my critical explication of the novel anyway.

However, Stephen's concerns with becoming and begetting, with creation and birth, which I have foregrounded, are clearly not confined to literary matters. At a philosophical level, those problems can be formulated in terms of theology, of history, of politics, while at the level at which Stephen primarily experiences them—that of an young man's dilemmas about his own future—they can act as a basis for possible identification even on the part of those readers who managed to escape all contamination by the adolescent image of oneself as future Major Writer.

Yet the germs of an implicit answer to at least some formulations of this general problem are indeed to be found in the very nature of the literary material before us. For if we ask how a possibility becomes actual, how a thought is born, where does the new come from, what is the basis of creation—is it from a void, a nothing from which *creatio ex nihilo* occurs, or from some preceding stuff, some material to be manipulated—then the very features of Stephen's style which encourage a certain sliding identification also act as indicators of a reply to that question: it is the multi-valent character of the words on the page, their capacity to be taken over and re-used with new meanings in their new contexts, which perhaps gives us some clue as to the nature of literary creation, of creativity.

We become very aware that our own attempt to write about Joyce also involves us in a re-writing of Joyce's own writing, not merely quotation but appropriation, not simply citation but a curious co-composition, even a kind of co-creation.

Yet that process of critical co-operation can indeed leave the reader of the criticism outside the circle of assimilation. It may still be useful, then, to attempt to offer, as a second try, a more accessible, more analytical, mode of commentary and explication. Part of the point of doing so, however, will be to return later to a consideration of how these two different modes (call them A and B modes, pehaps) of criticism may themselves be related in our understanding of Joyce's texts, how, in a sense, Joyce's work already anticipates the problem of having to choose between those modes of criticism, of writing.

Ulysses Algebra

If we ask what happpens in *Ulysses*, what's the story, we can reply—to be as banal as possible—that a Mr Leopold Bloom leaves home one morning and returns in the early hours of the following morning, bringing with him a certain Stephen Dedalus who had also 'left home' but in a more definitive sense; meanwhile, Mrs Molly Bloom has committed adultery with Blazes Boylan. Basically, that's it.

But we can immediately see that the three elements of the narrative singled out here are already variations on some ancient themes, on classically recurring patterns of narrative. The most obvious is that of the wanderer finally returning home (a homer), and the basic model of that is Homer's Ulysses in the *Odyssey*. That Joyce's *Ulysses* is a variation on Homer's *Odyssey* should need no full elaboration here, but we can take the connection as a starting point and try to develop it in a particular, limited, direction.

If we put the main characters of *Ulysses* and of the *Odyssey* in parallel, we get something like this:

FATHER	MOTHER	LOVER	SON
HUSBAND	WIFE		
BLOOM	MOLLY	BOYLAN	STEPHEN
ULYSSES	PENELOPE	SUITORS	TELEMACHUS

The *Odyssey* begins with Telemachus setting out to find his father Ulysses and if we take the suggested parallel seriously, we would have to say that Stephen finally finds his father in Bloom, and that Bloom finds his son in Stephen—and of course there is a great deal in the novel to support that view. But can we so easily compare Molly Bloom to Penelope? After all, the whole point about Penelope is that she does *not* commit adultery, but remains dutifully and faithfully waiting for Ulysses to return. That can hardly be said of Molly.

Stephen himself, of course, suggests a different literary model for our consideration. His much-talked-about theory of *Hamlet* suggests another set of four characters and another pattern of parallels, which would look something like this:

FATHER	ADULTERER	LOVER	SON
BLOOM	MOLLY	BOYLAN	STEPHEN
HAMLET snr	GERTRUDE	CLAUDIUS	HAMLET

There are difficulties here, of course. Hamlet senior is dead and only appears as a ghost, so how can we equate the solid fleshly Leopold Bloom with a ghost? Professor McHugh certainly does: as Bloom enters the Freeman's office in *Aeolus,* the professor murmurs 'The ghost walks', and it's worth noting that Bloom has just arrived from the cemetery where, like Ulysses in Book XI of the *Odyssey*, he has been visiting the dead. But we can leave that particular problem for a while and explore the role of *Hamlet* in *Ulysses* a little more.

Hamlet is introduced early. Twice in the first episode we are warned that Stephen will have something to say at length about Hamlet: 'Wait till you hear him on *Hamlet*' Buck Mulligan tells Haines, and later elaborates this to: ''He proves by algebra that Hamlet's grandson is Shakespeare's grandfather and that he himself is the ghost of his own father.'

Not only that, but *Ulysses* opens, like *Hamlet,* on battlements above the sea—though the two soldiers who precede the Ghost's appearance in *Hamlet* have to wait a long time for their appearance in *Ulysses.* They eventually turn up, appropriately, as the occasion for Bloom's final befriending of Stephen—as Private Compton and Private Carr in *Circe.* But that's a digression here.

It's the algebra of *Hamlet* that continues to preoccupy Stephen. In Mr. Deasy's classroom he offers us another variation: 'He proves by algebra that Shakespeare's ghost is Hamlet's grandfather.' But of course we have to wait for the full working out of this critical *aperçu* until we get to the even more appropriate setting of the National Library, in the episode which occupies the structural centre of the book: *Scylla and Charybdis* —though our appetite and awareness of *Hamlet* has perhaps been kept alive in the meanwhile by a conversation with a grave-digger in the *Hades* episode, by noting—with Bloom—that the actress Mrs. Bandman Palmer had once played Hamlet, and by asking—with Stephen—how Hamlet senior ever found out that his murderers 'In the porches of mine ear did pour' poison, since he died in his sleep—a question that perhaps shows too little respect for the powers of the dead. We can also note that Stephen wears a Hamlet hat.

Now, leaving aside these ornamentations (we'll come back to two of them), let us move to the National Library and take up an echo: the schoolboys in Mr. Deasy's school had wanted a ghost-story; now, in *Scylla and Charybdis*, John Eglinton reminds us that Stephen 'will have it that *Hamlet* is a ghoststory.' Stephen, ever analytical, first asks the highly pertinent question: 'What is a ghost?' and answers:

> One who has faded into impalpability through death, through absence, through change of manners. Elizabethan London lay as far from Stratford as corrupt Paris lies from virgin Dublin. Who is the ghost from *limbo patrum* returning to the world that has forgotten him? Who is King Hamlet?

Let me remind you simply of the bones of Stephen's answer. The actor who played the ghost of Hamlet's father was, we know, Shakespeare; Shakespeare's own son was called Hamnet, who had died, aged eleven, in 1596; *Hamlet* was written, when Shakespeare was 35, just after the death of his own father; Anne Hathaway was—still according to Stephen—an adulteress, the guilty Gertrude of the play, and her Claudius was none other than Shakespeare's brother Richard and/or his brother Edmund —perpetuated as villanous names in Shakespeare's other plays.

By a brilliant orchestration of challengeable facts and dubious dialectic, supported by lashings of local colour and vivid helpings of biographical detail, Stephen Dedalus inexorably establishes that the whole of Shakespeare's work is rooted in the circumstances of his own unsuccessful sexual career—from his seduction at the age of eighteen by the older woman Anne, to his substitutionary homosexual but foiled affection for the mysterious Mr W. H.

We can come back to some of the details and further elaborations later, but we can develop immediately one triple parallel, between the *Odyssey*, *Hamlet* and *Ulysses* or, more strictly, between the alleged relationships of Homer, Shakespeare, and James Joyce to their respective works.

The parallel between Shakespeare and Joyce is clear: just as Stephen Dedalus bases his interpretation of *Hamlet* on Shakespeare's life, so critics have always been tempted to base their readings of Joyce's work on Joyce's own life. And it is Joyce himself who has been very largely responsible for that temptation. Not only did he write *A Portrait of the Artist as a Young Man* —which could hardly fail to be taken as autobiography thinly disguised as a novel—but he has also left, in work-notes, letters and interpretative books written with his co-operation, enough apparent 'evidence' for us to seek—and find—autobiographical data embedded in *Ulysses*, the many thousands of echoes of his life which biographers can specify in the novel— from the location of the Martello Tower to the death of his mother, from the overall picture of the somewhat marooned writer returned from Paris to an indifferent and rather stifling Dublin, to such local details as the songs his father used to sing.

Anyone interested in pursuing such matters can read the 800 and more pages of Richard Ellmann's biography of Joyce.

But a somewhat less obvious parallel can also be drawn between Joyce's *Ulysses* and Homer's *Odyssey*. In *Ulysses* Joyce has presented us with enough information about Dublin—its streets, its shops, its pubs, its houses and hotels, as well as its people, many of them under their actual names—for a careful historian of later centuries to be able to reconstruct from the novel an extremely detailed account of life in Dublin in the early twentieth century. And one of the reasons why Joyce took the *Odyssey* as his major point of reference in *Ulysses* was that in the late nineteenth century it suddenly became a great deal clearer —or seemed to—that Homer's work was, after all, based on actual places. Two of the main influences on Joyce were the discovery and excavation of, it seemed, the real Troy by Heinrich and Sophie Schliemann, from about 1870 onwards, and, secondly, the researches of Samuel Butler and others into the geographical accuracy which underpins the *Odyssey*.

Suddenly, as a result of the excavations by the Schliemanns and their successors, we could see again the walls of Troy, walk round the area where the Greek camp had stood, enter the walls where the Trojan Horse came fatally in. Sophie Schliemann was even photographed wearing jewellery found at the site of Troy which might conceivably have been worn by the beautiful Helen herself. It was a bit like discovering the Garden of Eden, complete with half-chewed apple.

And then came Samuel Butler's investigations, in which he not only showed, in detail, that the various sites and apparently mythical places mentioned in the *Odyssey* had existed but that they could, like Schliemann's Troy, be visited by today's tourist. He printed photographs of where Ulysses had landed and met Nausicaa: his photograph was captioned, perhaps a little unromantically, 'View of the Salt Works at S. Cusumano'. Even more intriguingly—and, for classical scholars, outrageously—he sought to prove that the author of the *Odyssey* was in fact a woman. His book, published in 1897, was entitled: *The Authoress of the Odyssey*. And that was a bit like not only finding the broken tablets of the Ten Commandments at the foot of Mount Sinai, but deciphering the signature on them as 'Miss God'.

Joyce's *Ulysses* is clearly written with a full awareness of such researches, but more importantly with a full awareness of their significance for literary criticism: even Homer's epics were based on detailed material facts which were available for inspection; mythical Troy was as real and solid as dirty Dublin; the island of Calypso was as real as the Isle of Man. The classical mind could only boggle.

But, of course, after the initial shock, bathos awaited. At the end of Stephen's excavations into Shakespeare's love-life, John Eglinton asks him:

> —You have brought us all this way to show us a French triangle. Do you believe your own theory?
> — No, Stephen said promptly.

That resounding 'No' echoes through the novel with almost the same force as Molly's final, resounding 'Yes'.

If we want to grasp *Ulysses*, it might seem, the details of Joyce's life and the material facts of Dublin street-directories are as ultimately irrelevant as Shakespeare's laundry-bills for his second-best sheets to an understanding of *Hamlet*, or the bi-annual profit-loss accounts of the S. Cusumano salt works to an appreciation of the *Nausicaa* episode. A retracing of Odysseus's voyage would not necessarily improve one's writing style. Nor are the stones of Troy the words Homer sung.

Four Quartets

But—to start again—what certainly isn't irrelevant to *Hamlet* is that it isn't a French triangle. It's at least a quartet and behind it lies another quartet, one we also know from Homer. Some more algebraic permutations.

In Hamlet we have:

HAMLET GERTRUDE CLAUDIUS HAMLET JNR

Homer's *Odyssey* opens not immediately with Telemachus, the son in the previous equations, but with a history which includes a reference to another son, Orestes (Book I, line 30ff). Orestes is indeed a closer parallel to Hamlet than is Telemachus. Aeschylus's *Oresteia*, you may recall, also comprises a quartet:

AGAMMEMNON CLYTAEMNESTRA
AEGISTHUS ORESTES/ELECTRA

The message of the ghost (Agammemnon) in the *Oresteia* is to avenge his murder by killing his murderers, adulterous Clytaemnestra and lover-usurper Aegisthus. But that involves Orestes in having to kill his own mother—a rather harsher version of the task laid upon Hamlet, though as a result of his actions Gertrude does indeed die.

And, according to Buck Mulligan's aunt, Stephen Dedalus did in fact kill his mother:

—The aunt thinks you killed your mother, he said.
—Someone killed her, Stephen said gloomily.

The 'agenbite of inwit', the gnawings of guilty conscience, start there: his original sin is the 'murder' of his mother. But in the algebra of *Ulysses* we can hardly forget that, for Stephen, the 'original sin' that underlies all Shakespeare's work is incest—Anne's incestuous adultery with her husband's brother(s). But that is a mild case of incest compared with the original Greek triangle, the basic equation at the core of both myth and psychoanalysis. Behind the quartets of *Hamlet* and of the *Oresteia* lies the Oedipal triangle so beloved of the 'new Viennese school' which Stephen himself mentions:

LAIUS JOCASTA (OEDIPUS) OEDIPUS

Oedipus's fate is to kill his father and marry his mother, to become the father of his own grandchildren. But on the logic of that parallel or equation, if Stephen has been responsible for killing his mother, whom can he now marry but his father?

Let us retrace these simultaneous equations and their transformations. In *Hamlet* and in the *Oresteia* it is the father's ghost who appears, in effect enjoining 'Kill your mother'; but in *Ulysses* it is the mother's ghost who appears:

> In a dream, silently, she had come to him, her wasted body within its loose graveclothes giving off an odour of wax and rosewood, her breath bent over him with mute secret words, a faint odour of wetted ashes.

And in *Oedipus Tyrannos* Oedipus kills his father and marries his mother, whereas in *Ulysses* Stephen 'kills' his mother.

Therefore, on the logic of a transposed *Hamlet,* Stephen ought to kill his father. Whereas on the logic of a transposed *Oedipus*, Stephen ought to marry his father.

The latter possibility is actually toyed with in the text: Buck Mulligan interprets Bloom's interest in Stephen as homosexual: 'O, I fear me, he is Greeker than the Greeks'—the Greeks being perhaps the gayest society known to ancient civilisations—and 'He looked upon you to lust after you. O Kinch, thou art in peril. Get thee a breechpad.' But in so far as Bloom stands in for Stephen's father, that relationship has already been ruled out by Stephen himself:

> They are sundered by a bodily shame so steadfast that the criminal annals of the world, stained with all other incests and bestialities, hardly record its breach. Sons with mothers, sires with daughters, lesbic sisters, loves that dare not speak their name, nephews with grandmothers, jailbirds with keyholes, queens with prizebulls . . . .
> —What links them in nature? An instant of blind rut. Am I father? If I were?

That comment of Stephen's arises from a discussion of Shakespeare's alleged homosexuality, his love for the Mr. W.H. of the sonnets. And we have already seen that any translation of the works of an artist into evidence about his life has to be ruled out: 'No' said Stephen.

That Shakespeare wrote homosexual love poems does not mean that William Shakespeare was necessarily homosexual. All it means is that Shakespeare in his work can create himself as a homosexual, just as he can create himself as the ghost of Hamlet's father or as the adulterous Gertrude. The artist can create him-self or her-self male and female, the way God created 'man' (or so a certain literary ideology would have it). Actresses can play Hamlet, just as Elizabethan boys once played women, and even though the *Odyssey* might have all the stylistic marks of being written by a woman (according to Samuel Butler), that does not mean that Homer was a woman (at least not according to a chauvinist literary ideology). Joyce (that female name, as is his mis-name Augusta) acknowledged Butler's theory by writing the entire *Nausicaa* episode in the style of a simpering lady novelist.

But he also acknowledged the theory that the name 'Homer' might designate multiple authors by writing each episode in a different narrative style. And just because Joyce wrote Molly Bloom's final female soliloquy, that certainly doesn't mean that James Augusta Joyce was a woman. The artist, like Stephen on the beach, is perhaps a Proteus, assuming whatever shape or identity he (or she) pleases—or can—in the work. But where does that then leave us? Who is an artist if, to misquote Bloom, he is 'all suddenly someone else'?

Let us recap, before proceeding with our algebraic twists
Do you understand how to do them now? he asked

If you follow Stephen's approach to *Hamlet*, or Samuel Butler's approach to the *Odyssey*, which is also the biographical critic's approach to *Ulysses*, you endorse a 'materialist' explanation of the novel, an account which claims finally that the novel arises from the facts which 'caused' it, an apotheosis of a sociology of literature. But Stephen's resounding refusal of his own theory implies that you can't, in the end, finally account for a novel by those material explanations. You can most certainly find Calypso's island, but you will not meet Calypso herself on any actual island, and on June 16th 1904 you would not have found any Leopold Bloom as the occupant of 7 Eccles Street.

On the other hand, if you say 'No" to such materialist approaches, where does the novel come from? If what we can know about the novelist can never account for the work, how do we account for it? Are we implicitly relying upon some variation of creation out of nothing, a kind of magical mystery?

That problem, in one of its many variants, had already preoccupied several centuries of thinkers, in the theological conundrum of the Incarantion, and more mundanely in the question of the historicity of Jesus, both variations on the problem of how 'God' can be 'in history', that nightmare from which even He might try to escape..

Thus, Jesus of Nazareth is another figure in a quartet of characters, or rather in an eternal triangle and another woman:

FATHER SON HOLY GHOST MARY

If, on a certain algebraic and inevitably heretical reading of Trinitarian theology, the Ghost is the impregnator of Mary, but the Father is also the Ghost, then not only is the Father truly the Father *of* the Son, but, if also the Father *is* the Son, then the Son is the Father of Himself—and has conceived himself by his own mother: 'He Who Himself Begot'. Ancient controversies had racked the early church on precisely this conundrum: Arians, Sabellians, and the rest had tried their own failed equations. And the crucial test of orthodoxy had been hammered on this anvil. In *Ulysses* Haines's simple version of that test comes down to belief in creation from nothing. The only alternative would be the blasphemously unthinkable materialist, and mundane, explanation, that Mary was an adulterer, a deceiver of Joseph—the case put by Bloom's old Jewish father, that Mary was seduced by 'Panther, the Roman centurion'. This would, of course, make Jesus an illegitimate child—a notion that hovers around the *Hades* and the *Oxen* episodes.

But isn't all fatherhood a version of creation from nothing, a legal fiction, a story told by the mother? In ancient Irish law a mother might simply 'name' the father she preferred for her child. And isn't all human existence an arbitrary and mysterious matter, our identity not be explained in terms of pre-cedent existences, even our own. 'AE IOU' — but the molecules have all changed. I no longer I. I am changed from that which I then was, as Stephen (as he then was) had said in *Portrait.*

When the issue takes shape as the Oedipal triangle, in the relation of any I to its parentage, it can, in practice and perhaps in therapy, be resolved, by adding a fourth to the original triangle: the child, growing up, eventually finds its own substitute for the loved, impossible, parent-lover: the wife replaces the lost mother, the husband takes the place of the forbidden father. But this can happen only in time, only as the story develops: the unconscious desires remain irresolvable, locked in a diagram that is without time, permanent, irremoveable. The narrative can allow the possibility that Stephen, say, will replace Bloom, Boylan, and all the other lovers in Molly's sequence of desires; but the desires themselves will remain, generating and driving other narratives, permanently holding this one in its form and shape, endlessly re-working the equations and algebra of desire.

When the issue takes form as a matter of shaping, of telling stories, of writing the narratives of our desires, it can, as a matter of practice, be resolved by recognising that the writing that appears to come from nothing, in hard practice comes from a re-working of other narratives, other writings, remembered phrases, long-forgotten lines, repressed and repeated. The fundamental material of the writer is the imaginings of previous writers, the patterns of their previous productions, and most of all the very language of their makings, the words they too have worked upon. George Moore, discussing a portrait of himself as a young boy, in his *Memories of My Dead Life* (1906), can write: 'it is pleasing to think that I was once not as I am now.' James Joyce can make Stephen, in his *Portrait*, say: 'I was not myself as I am now, as I had to become', and in his *Ulysses*: 'that which I was is that which I am and that which in possibility I may come to be.' And so on.

It is deeply appropriate that the episode concerned with birth itself should be itself a history of language, a narrative of past styles. But this, like the Oedipal truce, is only a partial solution to our quest: dependence and debt take us back along the chain, like a navel cord or telephone line, but was there ever an unwritten Eden of literature, an origin of language itself, a naming of the un-named? Homer cannot, after all, be the first father of European literature; he too, or she too, or they too, had before-hand a grandfather and grandmother, a history of previous convictions.

If we conflate the Oedipal and the Authorial we perhaps can recognise that we create only by rebelling against the received law of the father, speaking in the name of the father, taking the place of the predecessor—but where was that place in the first place?

The problem of being in place at all, of having a role within these eternal triangles of desire and of displacement, seems interminable, a world without end. Faced with the fact of our existence, in history, within the chains and sequences which form and give form, we have, it can seem, only two fundamental options, if history is not to remain simply a nightmare without escape. In the logic of all the variations there remains one final solution: to eradicate, eliminate, kill, erase, not the mother or the father but the self, one-self, one's-self, in an act not of murder but of suicide—as Bloom's father desperately did. But then Hamlet's question returns, at the heart of the matter; and with it the warning: perchance to dream.

The other alternative, faced with another oft-told tale, another ordinary day of wanderings, of ancient repeated banalities of the flesh and spirit, is to affirm a resounding final 'Yes' : an affirmation of the perpetuation of the present, in all its actualities and eventualities, into a future. Perhaps through that partiuclar 'Yes' which changes the equations, restructures the algebra, once again, puts a new loop of reflexiveness into the consciousness of history, as a new relation of past to future is co-created, the 'Yes' which confirms, in choice but also by chance, a new conception, a new composite, a new creation: the unpredictable re-workings of combined genetic pasts, of grand-fathers and great-grandmothers, of all past Adams and Eves. Riverrun.

Yes. She said.

www.ingramcontent.com/pod-product-compliance
Lightning Source LLC
Chambersburg PA
CBHW051815050726
47598CB00006B/2563

* 9 7 8 1 9 1 0 9 5 6 0 1 4 *